Career Self-Management and Personal Branding

A strategic approach to developing superior skills and marketing them professionally

Valeri Chukhlomin, PhD

State University of New York
Empire State College

Career Self-Management and Personal Branding

A strategic approach to developing superior skills and marketing them professionally

Valeri Chukhlomin, PhD

UMB **Upward Mobility Books**

Career Self-Management and Personal Branding:

A strategic approach to developing superior skills and marketing them professionally. -160 p.

Published by Upward Mobility Books, Saratoga Springs, New York.
E-mail: info@upwardmobility.associates
ISBN-13: 979-8619535082

Library of Congress Control Number: 2020905956

Printed in the United States of America.

Previous edition:
Self-Management and Self-Marketing by Valeri Chukhlomin (2015)
ISBN-13: 978-1500837785

Contents

List of Figures

About the Book

Currently, there is a growing understanding of the necessity to embed career competencies and skill-building activities into the design of undergraduate and graduate degrees, particularly within the business and management environment. This book is intended for senior undergraduate and graduate students specializing in any area of business, management and economics, as it will help them better understand the process of professional development and master necessary skills, such as competitive job selection, job analysis, self-assessment, skills management, and developing effective strategies for self-improvement and self-marketing. Reading the book and taking the course can be also beneficial for managers and policy makers, as it is research-based and can provide insights into recent trends in workforce development in a global context.

The book is to accompany *"Career Self-Management and Self-Marketing",* a 4-credit, advanced level business course at the State University of New York's Empire State College. It is also used as a recommended text in the popular *"Career Brand Management"* specialization on "Coursera" designed to help learners develop their career-building skills. By the end of the course, the students will achieve the following learning goals:

- Learn how to approach and conduct job analysis and self-assessment in a competitive job market environment.
- Implement strategic management approach and use proven business strategy techniques for self-analysis and professional development.
- Identify professional and generic competencies and skills that are most valuable for their chosen field; collect evidence of their actual performance, measure it against benchmarks, and learn how to monitor progress.
- Use career self-management tools, such as self-assessment instruments, dashboards, e-portfolios.
- Integrate self-marketing and personal branding techniques for self-promotion.
- Develop active learning, metacognitive and self-regulatory skills.
- Get familiar with underpinning learning theories, such as self-regulated learning and transformative learning, to guide their professional development and personal growth.

Since the first edition in 2014, the instructional materials included in this book have been used by many hundreds of students at the State University of New York's Empire State College. At the same time, the course became a prototype for developing a highly successful *"Career Brand Management"* specialization on "Coursera", with close to 100,000 enrolled learners from around the globe. In the new edition, we revised and updated learning materials and activities, with an emphasis on self-coaching skills, so that the learners can continue building and strengthening their skills long after they have completed the course.

What Students Say About the Course

Dear Self-Management and Self-Marketing (BME-21424) Students! At the beginning of this course I was unaware of what this class entailed. I thought it was mostly about time management and how to market yourself in the business world. I was wrong, it turned out to be one of the most rewarding classes I have taken thus far in my college career. I learned about strategies, strengths, weaknesses, and opportunities within myself and my workplace. When I started this class in the Fall, I was a general manager of a store profiting about $15,000 per week. Unaware that I was using many of the techniques addressed in this course, I was able to expand upon my prior knowledge and increase sales and employee satisfaction within a few months. In the middle of this course, I was given the opportunity to apply for a district manager position within my network using many of the tools I learned in this class. I was told by my franchisee that I had one of the best interviews she has ever conducted. Although, I did not get that position, she saw my potential and I am now the general manager of the largest revenue store in our network. This course has given me the confidence I needed to take chances and show others what I am capable of. I look forward to using many of the tools used in this class to help my crew and better myself as a manager and self-directed learner. If you are looking for a class that will challenge you but help you learn more about yourself, this is the one to take. You will not regret it!

Sincerely,
Emily Baker

Self-Management and Self- Marketing was a wonderful course that I enjoyed taking this past semester. It taught me a lot about myself and the skills I need to have to succeed out in today's job market. I learned to be honest with myself and look at the skills that I am strong in and what I need to work on. I also learned how to promote myself to organizations out there so they can see that I am the best candidate. Students should take this course to learn how to strengthen their skills and learn how to use the tools that are out there to succeed. This course will help you grow educationally and professionally as well.

Sylvia Buccieri Cromwell

I took Dr. Valeri Chukhlomin's course called Self-Management & Self-marketing for my Spring 2019 semester. This course helped me explore my critical skills and assess progress by defining my strengths and weaknesses. I learned how to use valuable assessment tools and rubrics to quantify my competitive standing and reflect on what could be opportunities. These templates are essential for future goal setting, career planning and time management. What I loved the most about this course was learning the importance of measurement and the advantage it provides for creating better overall strategic thinking and decision-making. I will continue to use this knowledge in my self-development practice.

All best,
Suzanne Perez

Preface

Hello everyone and welcome to Career Self-Management and Self-Marketing! I am very excited to see you in the course and do hope that I can get to know all of you during the next several months. I am glad that you have selected this course and believe that you will find it useful for your career growth and personal development. Yes, indeed, the course is very successful, well attended, and usually highly regarded by students. This is what I hear all the time from those who have completed the course since it was first launched in 2015. Initially, I was thinking of a small-scale, experimental study, with may be 10-15 participants. Now, the course enrolls 2-3 full groups every term three times a year! Even more, there is now a non-credit clone of this course that is offered on Coursera, the leading online platform for professional development for global audiences, where close to 100,000 learners have taken it since 2016.

I think that the success of the course is based on the need of adult students to take an advanced level study in career development which would go far beyond introductory courses in self-awareness and the basics of job search. Particularly, for business students as they can learn how to use many of the management and marketing tools and techniques that they have learned in the college and their workplace for improving their own competitive standing in the job market. This is actually what I did by myself and for myself - and this is what I would like to tell you in the beginning of the course.

Two decades ago, I found myself in a situation where I had to relocate to another country and to basically start over my entire life. Upon transition, I was able to get some professional retraining and started applying for jobs, without much success, dozens and dozens of times. I knew that I was well-prepared, but it appeared that my applications were not scored highly enough. When they were, I seemed not to perform very well at job interviews. Or, there were better prepared and thus higher scoring candidates. Then, I started wondering about it and met with some recruiters who were specialized in my occupational area and also with people who had succeeded in their job applications in similar situations. What they all were saying was that I needed to learn how to better document and present my skills. Also, to learn more about the exact needs in the workplace I was applying for and to develop some new skills in case I was missing them. But, most importantly, they mentioned that I needed to find out how to better sell myself. This was completely mind blowing, because I had never seen it this way and I hated the very idea of self-selling. But what could I do? So, I forced myself to switch gears and to turn into a self-marketer. Eventually, I learned this life-saving skill and found a new and highly rewarding employment.

In my new place, Saratoga Springs, NY, I engaged in doing things that I thought I knew the best, namely, developing international programs, supervising a subset of the college's online program, teaching for MBA. I have also managed to climb all the steps in the academic ladder from an assistant to full professor, in a short time, because I think - in addition to sheer hard work - I already knew how to better prepare myself for career growth and job promotion. At the same time, I have been doing a lot of reading on talent management in the corporate world and studied career building and self-development from a research perspective. When teaching business strategies for MBA, I began exploring the idea of using strategic management tools for personal development with my students, and they loved it! In MBA programs, students do a lot of case studies, using examples of companies to illustrate the concepts and theories of strategic planning. What you do not see in a typical MBA program is how to use the same methods and tools for the only enterprise that (you think) you know well - the EnterpriseYOU!

Thinking about it and discussing career growth with MBA students actually convinced me that it would be great if I used my knowledge of business strategy and career-building to develop an innovative, advanced level course on career self-management for senior undergraduate and graduate business students. This is what I did, and it has proven to be working extremely well! I wish that I had taken a course like this years ago.

Basically, this is it. But here is one more thing. It turns out that learning about how to sell thyself is not the main outcome of the course. Similar to the corporate world, enhancing marketability is only the first step in transforming the business. The most crucial step is to use the marketing philosophy for developing new, superior capabilities and core competencies, so that the business can gain sustainable competitive advantage in the marketplace. The same appears to be true for career self-management. In order to market yourself professionally, you have to become a master of skills management. How much do you know about skills management? Do you want to know and learn how to use the knowledge in practice? In this course, you will find a lot of interesting readings about it and plenty of exercises. Are you ready to learn how to get skilled? Let's get started!

Professor Valeri Chukhlomin
Saratoga Springs, NY

Acknowledgments

The development of the course and the accompanying book is informed by more than three decades of teaching, mentoring, and research conducted by the author in Australia, China, Russia, and the United States. When working on the first edition of the book, I received highly valuable input from Professor Susan Oaks, Associate Professor John M. Beckem II, Interim Dean Dr. Ronnie Mather, and Adjunct Professors Suzanne Benno, Irina Chukhlomina, and Gene Dichiara. I would also like to express my sincere gratitude to my colleagues at the ESC's Center for Distance Learning, the School of Business, and the Graduate School for their continuous support and encouragement. On numerous occasions professional advice was kindly and generously provided by Professor Meg Benke and Professor Julie Gedro. Video production and instructional design were supported by the State University of New York's Empire State College and Innovative Instructional Technology Grants (IITG). To redesign the course for "Coursera", the production team included Associate Professor Michele Forte, Associate Professor John M. Beckem II, Associate Professor Dana Gliserman-Kopans, instructional designers Antonia Jokelova and Alena Rodick, videographer John Hughes, associate executive producer Amy Giaculli, and the author of this book. Very importantly, the development of the course wouldn't be possible without a highly enthusiastic response and an incredibly meaningful feedback provided by the students.

The Course at a Glance

Course Syllabus / Learning Contract

MRKT 4050 Career Self-Management and Self-Marketing
4 credits, advanced level

Course Description

This course introduces students to advanced topics in career self-management, individual skills management and development, self-marketing, and personal branding. It is designed for working, early-to-mid-career professionals looking for ways to enhance or change their careers. We expect that students in this course are already familiar with basic career development tools and job search techniques (resume, cover letter, job applications, and interviewing) and are interested in learning how to further enhance their career-building skills. Throughout the course, students will engage in a series of interlinked learning activities aimed at identifying, benchmarking, evaluating, peer-reviewing, documenting, presenting, and improving their job-related skills. They will learn how to use contemporary learning theories and powerful management and marketing tools and techniques for effective self-development and self-promotion. Recommended prerequisites: Marketing Principles and Principles of Management.

Assumptions and prerequisite knowledge

The course is developed with business students in mind. We expect that students in this course are typically working professionals who are already familiar with the foundations of career development. For example, they know how to write a resume and a covering letter, how to use a job search website and how to prepare for a job interview. We also expect that you have taken an introductory level career development course, or a short training focused on self-awareness. We think that you probably have established a LinkedIn profile, too. It may have happened that you have recently applied for a new job or a promotion and chances are that you didn't get it. Or, you have begun thinking about a career change. This is exactly the kind of situation where you would benefit the most from this course. We would like you to mobilize all your business knowledge (management, marketing, HR, strategy, information systems, psychology) and use it for your own personal development and growth. We would like you to think about this course as a personal strategy capstone and, therefore, we will be treating you as a C.E.O. (Chief Executive Officer) of EnterpriseYOU. Of course, as a human being, you are unique. But in this course, we assume that you have already discovered that there is a lot of competition out there where many people have possessed similar skills. We think that you have probably decided that you should seriously focus on your portfolio of job-related skills. And what you are likely to have also discovered is that you really need to maximize the market value of your skills portfolio to get the job or promotion you want. If so, this is the right time to take this course.

Course-level Learning Outcomes

CO1	Examine learning theories, such as positive psychology, self-directed learning, active regulation, goal setting, situated and transformational learning, and apply them for effective career self-management, skill-building, and career growth in the context of a competitive, skill-based job market environment.
CO2	Analyze strategic management tools and techniques and implement them for scanning competitive job market environments and developing effective personal strategies for skill-building and career growth.
CO3	Utilize performance management methodologies and tools to identify, analyze, and objectively evaluate job-related competencies and skills.
CO4	Develop an ability to quantify your level of skills acquisition and objectively estimate the likely total skillset score for a given job in a competitive job selection process.
CO5	Use strategic marketing approach for collecting, organizing, peer-reviewing, and demonstrating evidence of your mastery of skills for successful job search/promotion.
CO6	Synthesize self-management and self-marketing methods and techniques for data-driven self-programming and effective skill-building training interventions.
CO7	Utilize information technology and active self-regulation for managing your skills portfolio and maintaining an effective career development workflow.

How the course is structured

The course is divided into seven modules. The recommended length of modules (for a 15-week term) is as follows:

- **Module M1**: Introduces the concept of career self-management and examines the theme of employability, skills, and career growth (weeks 1-2).
- **Module M2**: Examines individual skills management in a competitive job market environment (weeks 3-4)
- **Module M3**: Explores competencies and skills, skills analysis, and self-assessment (weeks 5-7)
- **Module M4**: Engages students in organizing and managing their personal skills lab (weeks 8-10)
- **Module M5**: Applies self-marketing and personal branding methods for self-promotion (weeks 11-13)
- **Module M6**: Synthesizes methods and techniques of active self-regulation (weeks 14-15 minus the very last day)

- **Module M7**: Engages in self-reflection and helps establishing a process for ongoing self-improvement in the future (the last day of the course).

Each Module contains a set of learning activities that typically include: 1) reading the content guide in the course, this textbook, and recommended articles; 2) watching optional instructional videos; 3) participating in the class discussion; 4) working on an e-portfolio task; 5) working on a written assignment. Students are required to participate in learning activities from the first day of each Module and submit all work by the last day of the Module. Typically, in each Module the due date for the corresponding e-portfolio task and assignment is the last day of the Module. Requirements for e-portfolio tasks are specified in the Career Self-Management e- Portfolio and Learning Journal Workbook template. Requirements for assignments are explained in Modules.

A note for ESC students: Using this course to meet requirements for Educational Planning credit

Empire State College students can use this course to fulfill the College requirements for Educational Planning credit. However, students must keep in mind that the course is not focused on developing their degree plan. Prior to taking this course, students are **strongly advised** to discuss the format of degree planning with their mentors. (For example, for working on a degree plan with the mentor a student may need to take a separate Educational Planning course).

As an elective, advanced level study within the Business, Management and Economics (BME) area of studies, this course will be useful for BME students in any concentration. Depending on the individual degree program design, the course can be placed either as part of concentration, or general learning. During the course, students will be required to present and evaluate concrete evidence of essential skills in all areas specified in the BME general guidelines; this activity is intended to strengthen the students' focus on learning outcomes of their college studies. This study can be taken at any point during the degree provided that prerequisite requirements are met. Students can discuss issues of timing with mentors. The advantage of taking it earlier (and before they finalize their degree plans) is that the student will be better prepared to identify and evaluate their essential skills' gaps and then calibrate their ESC studies to address those deficiencies and build a stronger competency base. The advantage of taking it at a later stage is that they will have the opportunity to evaluate their overall progress and think proactively about their future self-improvement and career goals, including, but not limited to, graduate study.

"Coursera": Supplementary instructional videos

Coursera and this course

Coursera (www.coursera.org) is a world leading online platform for professional development, with more than 40 million subscribed learners around the globe. Coursera is highly selective and only leading universities and major tech companies offer certified courses for Coursera subscribers. It is a fee-based service where tuition fees are covered by either subscribed businesses, or learners themselves. In 2015, a SUNY Empire State College team led by Professor Val Chukhlomin participated in a Coursera-led call for proposals to develop a career development specialization (= a sequence of short online courses) for the worldwide audience and won the competition. As a result, a new specialization called "*Career Brand Management*" was created and launched in 2016. Since then, close to 100,000 learners from around the globe have taken it. Later, the specialization received a nomination for the best online career development course by Reimagine-Education, the Oscar in the Higher Education Innovation.

How different is this course from the specialization on Coursera?

This course is a prototype for the specialization on Coursera. Meaning that the main ideas of this course were utilized when developing the project on Coursera. But there are many differences, too. This course is a credit-bearing educational activity; upon completion, you will receive 4 advanced level credits towards your degree at ESC. The specialization courses on Coursera are not credit-bearing; upon completion, learners receive a certificate. Also, Coursera is mainly a video-based platform; so, there are 150+ instructional videos that we created for the specialization. In addition, there are case studies, different readings, and exercises. Coursera learners are typically those with bachelor's degrees (40%) and masters (38%).

Does it make sense for students in this course to get access to the Career Brand Management specialization on Coursera?

Yes, it does but it is completely optional. So, what are the benefits? First of all, Coursera is specifically created for skill-building activities and you may find that getting familiar with Coursera can be highly useful for you in the future. So, it is a good idea to set up a Coursera account and try using it right now. Second, during this course Empire State College students can get free access to "Career Brand Management" specialization on Coursera. Thirdly, there are high quality learning resources (most importantly, instructional videos) that you may find beneficial as an additional learning resource for this course. Finally, you can get extra credit for using Coursera.

There is also an advanced level version of this course on "Coursera"!

Besides the specialization, in 2018 the College has launched yet another career development course on Coursera ("How to Get Skilled"). The new course is designed as a refresher and it targets more advanced level learners, typically those with already master level degrees, who are interested in further improving their skills. For this new course Professor Val Chukhlomin wrote a new book (also available on Kindle). You may consider taking that advanced level course in the future.

My Courses | Course Catalog

Learn New Skills at Your Own Pace

There's still time to enroll in **Career Brand Management.** Get started today.

Career Brand Management

The State University of New York

4-course Specialization

Enroll Now

You will learn from: The State University of New York

The State University of New York, with 64 unique institutions, is the largest comprehensive system of higher education in the United States. Educating nearly 468,000 students in more than 7,500 degree and certificate programs both on campus and online, SUNY has nearly 3 million alumni around the globe.

The State University of New York's Empire State College was created over 40 years ago with the mission to use innovative and flexible approaches to higher education that transform people and communities by connecting individuals' unique and diverse lives to their personal learning goals.\nOn the photo: SUNY Administration (image credits: Felix Lipov / Shutterstock.com)

Module Level Learning Objectives and Activities

	Module Level Learning Objectives	Learning Activities
M1	**(P) Personal Strategy for Effective Career Self-Management:** **How to develop a strategic orientation and begin planning for long-term career success** The innovative approach we have developed for this course is called the Contextual Advancement of Individual Skills for Sustainable Competitive Advantage (CAISSA). Drawing on the models and tools derived from business strategy (like SWOT analysis, VRIO, Competitive Analysis), we are asking you to imagine what it would be like if you were a C.E.O. of EnterpriseYOU charged with designing and implementing a winning personal strategy to gain a competitive edge in a skill-based, job competition. In this introductory Module you will identify the need for effective career self-management in the contemporary workplace, review your prerequisite knowledge and career-building skills, and examine theoretical foundations of self-directed learning and career development for working professionals. You will begin the Module with a discussion of employability in the context of a skill-based, competitive job market environment. Then, you will get familiar with the 7-step PSALTER process for effective career self-management that we use in the course. As a practical application, you will review and begin using some of the effective approaches to self-regulated career development, such as reflective learning, e-journaling, and career e-portfolio.	
M1-1	Review and discuss the concept of employability and employability skills for career success in a skill-based, competitive job market environment.	**D1**
M1-2	Review prerequisite knowledge, skills, and your readiness for this course including basic career development and job search techniques (resume, cover letter, job applications, and interviewing).	**A1-1**
M1-3	Examine some of the available resources preparing job applicants and career builders for skill-based, competitive job selection/promotion processes.	**D1, R1**
M1-4	Review and reflect on protean and boundaryless career orientations, career adaptability, and career growth scenarios.	**R1, CPW1**
M1-5	Identify and review your career self-management and career competencies (=career building skills).	**A1-2**
M1-6	Set up your career e-portfolio.	**CPW1**
M1-7	Set up your learning e-portfolio and reflective journal.	**CPW1**

M2	**(S) Individual Skills Management:** **How to utilize a business strategy approach to effectively self-manage your skills portfolio** This course is developed with business students in mind who can benefit from utilizing their management and marketing knowledge and skills for developing and executing a sound personal strategy. The goal of this Module is to examine strategic management tools and techniques, such as SWOT analysis and competitive analysis, for guiding career development activities in competitive job market environments. Similar to strategic planners in the corporate world who use SWOT analysis to develop the company's key competencies and to eventually achieve a competitive advantage, strategically oriented career builders can utilize business strategy for achieving a competitive edge in the skill-based job market environment. To do so, you will initially engage in a conversation about the applicability of the SWOT analysis for career growth. Then, as a practical application, we will ask you to engage in a realistic simulation of a competitive job selection process in your area of expertise/interest. First, acting as an employer, you will prepare a set of skill-based selection criteria for a given position. Then, acting as a prospective employee, you will address the selection criteria and prepare a detailed selection criteria statement. After that, you will switch back to the employer's role, thoroughly examine and evaluate the resultant selection criteria statement, and discuss it with your peers.	
M2-1	Identify methods and techniques originally developed for business strategy in the corporate environment that can be used for planning a sound personal strategy in a competitive job market environment.	**R2, D2**
M2-2	Identify your generic, professional, and personal skills.	**CPW2**
M2-3	Apply SWOT Analysis for analyzing your job-related skills and discuss your findings with the peers.	**CPW2, D2**
M2-4	Working in a simulated workplace environment, identify a required skillset and develop corresponding selection criteria for prospective candidates.	**A2-1**
M2-5	Responding to the selection criteria, prepare a mock selection criteria statement.	**A2-2**
M3	**(A) Self-Audit and Skills Analysis:** **How to use performance management techniques to analyze and evaluate your job-related skills.** The goal of this (and the following) Module is to learn how to utilize performance management methodologies, originally developed in the	

	corporate world, for skills assessment and individual skills management. To accurately measure and monitor the level of skills acquisition in a competitive job market environment, you will first need to learn how to operationalize skills and quantify the level of skills acquisition so that you can realistically estimate a total skillset score for each job-specific skillset. To do so, we will be using tools and techniques derived from human resource management. Topics in this Module include competency frameworks, units and elements of competency, critical tasks, mastery of performance, benchmarking, skills assessment, expert and peer assessment, and self-assessment. In the end of the Module, you will use Critical Skills Assessment Tool to analyze, and objectively evaluate the level of your mastery in one or several job-related, critical skill areas.	
M3-1	Examine performance management concepts and methodologies, such as competency frameworks, units and elements of competency, critical tasks, and discuss their applicability for individual skills management.	**R3**
M3-2	Critically review and analyze the selection criteria statement that you created in the previous Module and try to guestimate your likely skillset score in a job competition for the position you specified.	**D3**
M3-3	Identify the critical tasks that can be used for evaluating your mastery of skills for the chosen position.	**CPW3**
M3-4	Review the concept of benchmarking as used in the corporate world and examine its applicability for individual skills management.	**R3, CPW3**
M3-5	Identify benchmarks, assessment methods and tools for skills assessment in the above exercise.	**CPW3**
M3-6	Conduct self-assessment of your skills using the provided Critical Skills Assessment Tool (CSAT).	**A3-1**
M3-7	Examine your findings in light of the relevant competency frameworks and skill assessment methodologies.	**A3-2**
M4	**(L) Managing Your Skills Lab:** **How to objectively evaluate your T.S.S. (the Total Skillset Score).** In this Module, we will continue learning how to use performance management tools and techniques for individual skills management. The goal of the Module is to quantify your level of skills acquisition and learn how to objectively estimate your likely T.S.S. (The Total Skillset Score) for a given job in a competitive job selection process. In the beginning of the Module, you will examine theoretical and practical approaches to identifying and analyzing job-related skillsets. Then, you will continue exploring the use of performance management techniques for skills assessment. As a result, you will be able to quantify your level of skills acquisition for the chosen position and come up with a realistic estimate for your likely T.S.S. supported by the Critical Skills	

	Dashboard. In addition, you will create a process for: 1) collecting evidence of your mastery in performing job-specific skills; 2) soliciting and documenting expert and peer-assessment of the level of your skills acquisition. In the end of the Module, we will ask you to review your Critical Skills Dashboard and compare it with the results of your prior SWOT analysis. As self-assessment is the most convenient but the least objective method of skills assessment, we will ask you to think about how to make your self-assessment more accurate, valid, and reliable.	
M4-1	Review theoretical and practical approaches to identifying and analyzing job-related skillsets.	**R4**
M4-2	Continue working on the implementation of performance management methods and techniques for the quantification of your level of skills acquisition as related to the identified skillset for the chosen position.	**CPW4**
M4-3	Engage in the process of skills assessment by soliciting peer- and expert evaluation and conducting self-assessment of the skills in your skillset for the chosen position.	**D4, CPW4**
M4-4	Develop a process for collecting evidence of your mastery in performing job-specific skills and soliciting and documenting expert and peer-assessment of the level of your skills acquisition.	**CPW4**
M4-5	Synthesize and review your findings in the Module using the provided Critical Skills Dashboard, calculate and analyze your T.S.S.	**A4-1**
M4-6	Review theoretical foundations of self-assessment and reflect on your experience in self-assessing your skills.	**A4-2**
M5	**(T) Transformation:** **How to effectively present your mastery of skills and market yourself professionally.** The goal of this Module is to learn how to create, collect, organize, and exhibit artifacts demonstrating evidence of your mastery of skills for successful job search/promotion. You will examine methods and techniques originally developed for professional services marketing and promotion of human brands. As self-marketing is a complex career competency in itself, you will begin the Module by examining the underpinning knowledge, skills, and attitudes. Then, you will focus on developing mastery in documenting your skills and communicating them to various audiences using networking and impression management. Drawing on models, methods, and techniques derived from strategic marketing, you will establish a process for identifying and documenting your skills and practice in showcasing and communicating them in the form of an elevator pitch on You Tube.	

M5-1	Review theoretical foundations of professional services marketing and human branding and discuss their applicability for establishing and promoting your Professional Brand (The Skilled Self).	**R5, D5**
M5-2	Analyze self-marketing and personal branding as a key career competency (The 7P Framework) in the context of a competitive job selection and formulate a sound self-promotional strategy.	**CPW5**
M5-3	Analyze your self-marketing capability as a job-related skill by identifying and self-assessing underlying competency units/elements and critical tasks.	**CPW5**
M5-4	Develop Self-Marketing and Personal Branding Plan.	**A5-1**
M5-5	Apply the relevant elements of marketing communications mix for creating an elevator pitch on You Tube.	**A5-2**
M5-6	Synthesize elements of your self-promotional strategy and incorporate them into a functional resume and a LinkedIn professional profile (optional).	**CPW5**
M6	**(E) Effective Self-Regulation:** **How to effectively set and achieve your skill-building and self-promotional goals** The goal of this Module is to learn how to synthesize all self-management and self-marketing methods and techniques that we have learned in the course for effective self-programming and reaching your skill-building goals. You will begin by examining learning theories of self-directed learning, active regulation, goal setting, and feedback-seeking behavior. As a practical application, you will engage in peer reviewing of student elevator pitch presentations prepared in the previous Module. Then, you will review a popular SMART goals technique and examine ways of utilizing it for guiding your skill-building activities. After that, you will focus on developing your data-driven, evidence-based, and results-oriented professional development plan (PDP) and planning self-administered training interventions.	
M6-1	Examine learning theories of self-directed learning, active regulation, goal setting, and feedback-seeking behavior.	**R6**
M6-2	Examine peer review techniques and discuss the usefulness of feedback seeking behaviors.	**D6**
M6-3	Critically review a popular SMART goals technique and examine ways of utilizing it for guiding your skill-building activities to maximize your likely total skillset score in a competitive job selection context.	**R6, CPW6**
M6-4	Develop a data-driven, evidence-based, and results-oriented skill-building plan (SBP).	**A6-1**
M6-5	Plan a series of self-administered training interventions and active behaviors to achieve your skill-building and career growth goals.	**A6-1**

M6-6	Evaluate your results in this course and gains in career competencies and the underpinning knowledge base.	**A6-2**
M7	**(R) Reaching Career Goals: Review, Reflect, Revise, Reinforce, and Reinvigorate** **How to organize and sustain an effective career development workflow** The goal of this one-day Module is to review your progress in the course and prepare to sustain your career building effort in the future. In the beginning of the Module, you will review the results, reflect on your career competencies, and evaluate your level of self-confidence in implementing the methods and techniques that you have learned in the course. Then we will introduce you to the theme of ongoing self-coaching and propose a technique that may be helpful for you to organize and maintain an effective career self-management workflow in the future.	
M7-1	Review your progress in the course, reflect on your career competencies, and evaluate your level of self-confidence in implementing the methods and techniques that you have learned in the course.	**A7**
M7-2	Review self-coaching techniques in light of the learning theories and career self-management methodologies examined in the course.	**R7**
M7-3	Identify and examine information technologies that can be used to effectively organize and maintain your career self-management workflow.	**CPW7**

Learning activities:
R – Readings; **D** – Discussions, **A** – Assignments, **CPW** – Career Self-Management E-Portfolio and Workbook tasks.

Content guides

Module M1

Career Self-Management: Your Personal Strategy for Career Success

Overview

This is a short, two-week introductory Module. The overarching goal is to examine and discuss the concept of career self-management and the central role career self-management plays in skills acquisition and career growth. We would like you to develop a strategic orientation and begin planning for long-term career success.

The innovative approach we have developed for this course is called the Contextual Advancement of Individual Skills for Sustainable Competitive Advantage (CAISSA). Drawing on the models and tools derived from business strategy (like SWOT analysis, VRIO, Competitive Analysis), we are asking you to imagine what it would be like if you were a C.E.O. of EnterpriseYOU charged with designing and implementing a winning personal strategy to gain a competitive edge in a skill-based, job competition. In this introductory Module you will identify the need for effective career self-management in the contemporary workplace, review your prerequisite knowledge and career-building skills, and examine theoretical foundations of self-directed learning and career development for working professionals. You will begin the Module with a discussion of employability in the context of a skill-based, competitive job market environment. Then, you will get familiar with the 7-step PSALTER process for effective career self-management that we use in the course. As a practical application, you will review and begin using some of the effective approaches to self-regulated career development, such as reflective learning, e-journaling, and career e-portfolio.

Module Learning Objectives:

M1-1	Review and discuss the concept of employability and employability skills for career success in a skill-based, competitive job market environment.	**D1**
M1-2	Review prerequisite knowledge, skills, and your readiness for this course including basic career development and job search techniques (resume, cover letter, job applications, and interviewing).	**A1**
M1-3	Examine some of the available resources preparing job applicants and career builders for skill-based, competitive job selection/promotion processes.	**R1**
M1-4	Review and reflect on protean and boundaryless career orientations, career adaptability, and career growth scenarios.	**R1, CPW1**
M1-5	Identify and review your career self-management and career competencies (=career building skills).	**A1**
M1-6	Set up your career e-portfolio.	**CPW1**
M1-7	Set up your learning e-portfolio and reflective journal.	**CPW1**

Why are skills so important in the 21st century?

Actually, this is a very good question, that's why we decided to leave it for discussion **D1**. When looking for answers, you should use business media (*The Wall Street Journal*, *Fortune*, *Forbes*, and *The Economist*) to find out about specialists' opinion on the topic and then formulate your own judgment. Throughout this course, we'll be relying on the results obtained by researchers in this and other countries to substantiate and illustrate our statements and provide you with food for thought. For example, to understand the most recent emphasis on skills and skill gaps, we recommend that you read an excellent article by Denise Jackson "An international profile of industry-relevant competencies and skill gaps in modern graduates" published in the *International Journal of Management Education*, 2009, vol. 8(3), pp. 29-58.

As you can see in the above article, employers across Australia, Canada, UK, US and other developed countries express concerns about growing skill gaps. Interestingly enough, according to the researchers' report employers are less concerned with gaps in discipline-specific skills and are more focused on the lack of so called basic, soft and meta-skills. You can read more about it in another article "The Future of Marketing Education: A Practitioner's Perspective" written by David Finch, John Nadeau and Norm O'Reilly for *Journal of Marketing Education*, 2013, vol. 35(1), pp. 54-67. The article that is very interesting and well worth reading.

TIP: How to deal with recommended research articles and make sense of your findings

Here is an advice regarding reading research papers. If you do not have experience with research papers, you may think that reading 6-7 papers per week can be overwhelming. Actually, if you deal with lengthy papers, you may probably need more than a week to attentively read and fully digest just one paper. But fortunately, in most cases reading can be done much faster. If you are not specifically interested in learning about the research methodology used, you can skip it and only read the abstract, introduction and findings. This won't take a lot of your time and will give you a clear idea about what the authors studied and accomplished. Sometimes, you'll need to quickly browse the paper to look for theoretical frameworks, literature review, and interim results. For example, in the above-mentioned article we recommend you review an excellent list of meta-skills compiled by the authors.

TIP: How to summarize and report your findings

After reading or just browsing an article, it is a good idea to write down a paragraph with your notes and correctly cite the article. You will need it for your discussion, e-portfolio, and assignments. For example, after reading the above article (Finch et al, 2013), you could summarize the reading in the following way:

The authors of the paper studied the gap that had developed between knowledge-based curricula and practical needs and asked marketing practitioners in Canada about the gaps in education they found in recent marketing graduates. Surprisingly, those were not highly praised professional marketing skills that graduates were lacking; instead, foundational meta-skills (communication, time management, team work, problem solving, interpersonal, decision making, leadership) were found to be: a) the most desirable and valued by the employers; b) significantly underdeveloped in graduates (Finch et al, 2013).

Employability Skills

It is now time to review closely a broad range of skills that are mentioned in the above research articles. The common name for these skills is *Employability Skills.* A foundational research on employability skills was undertaken by the Business Council of Australia and the Australian Chamber of Commerce and Industry back in 2002. The authors defined employability skills as *'skills required not only to gain employment, but also to progress within an enterprise so as to achieve one's potential and contribute successfully to enterprise strategic directions.'* The report resulted in developing a framework for employability skills (DEST, 2002). The authors of the report identified personal attributes required for the 21st century employees and came up with a list of eight employability skills.

The eight identified skills that were found to be the most relevant to both entry-level and established employees were the following:

- **Communication skills** that contribute to productive and harmonious relations between employees and customers.
- **Teamwork skills** that contribute to productive working relationships and outcomes.
- **Problem solving skills** that contribute to productive outcomes.
- **Self-management skills** that contribute to employee satisfaction and career growth.
- **Planning and organizing skills** that contribute to long-term and short-term strategic planning.
- **Technology skills** that contribute to effective execution of tasks.
- **Life-long learning skills** that contribute to ongoing improvement and expansion in employee and company operations and outcomes.
- **Initiative and enterprise skills** that contribute to innovative outcomes.

In more detail, the above mentioned employability skills are characterized by Denise Jackson on p. 348 in her article "Business undergraduates' perceptions of their capabilities in employability skills: Implications for industry and higher education" (*Industry and Higher Education*, 2012, Vol.26(5), October, pp. 345-356).

Interestingly, some forward-thinking researchers described employability skills 30 years ago! For example, an excellent introduction to the topic was written by Anthony Carnevale, Leila Gainer and Ann Meltzer in their book "Workplace basics: The essential skills employers want" (Jossey-Bass: San-Francisco, 1990). Even today, this is still one of the best foundational sources on employability skills. Later in the course you will get familiar with the modern thinking on employability in light of skill-based job competition.

Maintaining Employability in the 21 Century

This is all about how to manage oneself!

There are thousands of publications, YouTube videos, and TED talks dealing with employability and 21st century careers. The bottom line is that the way to develop employability and career skills and design a unique career pathway is up to the individual. In these introductory weeks, we recommend that you get familiar with the following, freely available publications.

"This is the real reason new graduates can't get hired" by Ronald Alsop. 19 November 2015. Available at: http://www.bbc.com/capital/story/20151118-this-is-the-real-reason-new-graduates-cant-get-hired.

In this BBC Capital online publication, the author discusses the reason that many employers say that "*today's university graduates don't quite measure up*". According to CareerBuilder, an online job search site, recent graduates lack problem-solving, creative thinking, and interpersonal skills. According to another survey by the Association of American Colleges and Universities, there is a big gap between students' perceptions and employers' expectations. For example, 62% of students think that they are well prepared in oral communications versus 28% of employers; similar numbers are reported in quantitative skills (55% versus 28%), teamwork (64% versus 23%), problem-solving (59% versus 23%), and applying knowledge to real life problems (59% versus 23%). Yet another survey by YouthNet, a UK organization, found that "*almost half of young applicants don't understand required job skills, and about two thirds of employers reject candidates because they cannot clearly articulate their abilities*". While redesigning curricula might mitigate the problem, jobseekers must do their part to better prepare for 21st century careers and take every opportunity to craft and document required skills using internships, volunteer work, and career development activities.

"Career planning: the second time around" by John Mullins. *Occupational Outlook Quarterly*, Summer 2009. Available at: http://www.bls.gov/careeroutlook/2009/summer/art02.pdf

The author, an economist in the Office of Occupational Statistics and Employment Projections, the U.S. Bureau of Labor Statistics (BLS), discusses a range of problems associated with career change. According to data from the BLS, Americans change jobs fairly often – about every 5 years. Changing a career is different from switching jobs; it means leaving an established occupation and embarking on a completely new one. The author provides advice for potential career changers by describing necessary steps in career planning. Those steps include assessing your current situation, assessing yourself, developing career fitness, and finding information. The article presents useful sources for career changers, including the Occupational Outlook Handbook, the Occupational Outlook Quarterly, the Occupational Information Network, etc.

Dr. Tracey Wilen-Daugenti's blog. *The Huffington Post.* Available at: **http://www.huffingtonpost.com/dr-tracey-wilendaugenti/**

The author, a prominent scholar and writer, who held leadership positions at Apple, HP, Cisco Systems and the Apollo Group, regularly publishes on the theme of career development in the 21st century. Her posts are brief, informative, thought-provoking, and highly energetic. Topics include IT jobs, careers for women, job hunting, career development lessons, career branding, and many others. One particular blog, called "*Career Branding: How to Market Yourself Well*", posted by Dr. Wilen-Daugenti on April 5, 2013, is especially relevant for this course. It is accessible at: http://www.huffingtonpost.com/dr-tracey-wilendaugenti/career-branding_b_3009930.html.

"***Career advising in a VUCA Environment***" by Leigh S. Shaffer and Jacqueline M. Zalewski. *NACADA Journal, vol. 31(1), Spring 2011*, 64-74. A pdf version is available at: http://dx.doi.org/10.12930/0271-9517-31.1.64.

"***A Human Capital Approach to Career Advising***" by Leigh S. Shaffer and Jacqueline M. Zalewski. *NACADA Journal, vol. 31(1), Spring 2011*, 75-87. A pdf version is available at: http://www.nacadajournal.org/doi/abs/10.12930/0271-9517-31.1.75.

The authors discuss challenges facing career developers and career advisors in volatile, uncertain, complex and ambiguous (VUCA) environments and provide a framework of critical success factors for developing the 21st century career building skills. The framework includes the following requirements for career developers:

- Maintain your employability.
- Be proactive, develop a positive attitude.
- Increase your human capital by developing transferable skills.
- Develop capabilities to acquire new skills on your own.
- Learn how to document and communicate new skills.
- Engage in self-marketing.

When working on this course, we utilized and further developed the above framework.

"**Managing Oneself**" by Peter Drucker. From *Management Challenges for the 21st Century*, Butterworth-Heinemann, 2004, 161-195. Reprinted in *Harvard Business Review Press*, January 2008. A pdf version is available at: http://academic.udayton.edu/lawrenceulrich/LeaderArticles/Drucker%20Managing%20Oneself.pdf

The author, a prominent management thinker, educator, consultant and writer, explains why in the 21st century one needs to be his/her own chief executive officer (C.E.O) – and what it actually means. This is a must read for anyone interested in career self-management.

VIDEO LECTURE: Strategic Career Self-Management

In 2016, an extended version of this course was videotaped for the worldwide audience and is now used by dozens of thousands of career builders on Coursera.org. We think that you may find some of the videos very useful. For example, in the following video we discussed how the skill of managing oneself is similar to the requirements for being a C.E.O. (chief executive officer). We call it a C.E.O. of EnterpriseYOU.

© Text: Val Chukhlomin. Narration: Amy Giaculli. Image credits: Shutterstock.com.

Please note that in this and other videos we refer to courses in the Coursera's Career Brand Management specialization. The specialization follows the same logic as this course, though the sequence of activities is slightly different.

Hello again! In this presentation we'll review the first course in this specialization, Strategic Career Self-Management. To begin let me clarify why we named it Strategic Career Self-Management with a subtitle, A Skill to Get Skilled.

The term Career Management is often used to describe workforce development programs undertaken by corporations or public organizations and aimed at managing the careers of their employees. For individuals interested in climbing the corporate ladder career management provided by organizations can be really helpful. But having someone else manage your career can be risky, especially when, keeping in mind, that these days individuals must change careers often. There's a huge benefit in learning how to self-manage your career.

The term Career Self-Management is used to capture an individual's perspective on career planning and development. Career self-management is what an individual can and should do in order to be in charge of his or her own career. A tactical approach to career self-management deals with short-term planning and immediate actions. For example, taking a Coursera course in business analytics to add a certificate to your resume for a job interview next month.

A strategic approach to career self-management focuses on long-term career planning decisions. For example, setting career goals, obtaining a degree, entering a profession, or launching a new business. In this course, we suggest that you adhere to a long-term strategic approach to career self-management. Using business terminology, you may see yourself as a kind of enterprise in a competitive environment where critical success factors are your skills and your brand. In acting as the CEO of your enterprise you must design and implement the best possible strategy that will bring you from your current situation to where you want to be.

Now, if we go back to recommendations for career success in literature, we can see that the first two critical success factors are related to embracing the role of the CEO in the EnterpriseYou. In the course, we'll discuss various aspects of being a CEO, including self-organization and self-control. In terms of self-strategy development, you were supposed to set your career goals. This is outside of the course. But once they are established, career goals will help you design your future work self and identify required competencies and skills within the course.

Increasing one's human capital by developing transferable skills is the central idea of career self-management as recommended by researchers and practitioners [1]. To take on this you, as the CEO of EnterpriseYou, will need to know what skills you need to develop, in what degree, and how to measure results and monitor progress. But before engaging in the business of skill building, you may want to find out why getting skilled is so important for career success in the current job market.

According to Gallup research [2], only 11% of American business leaders strongly agree with the statement that higher education institutions in this country are graduating students with the skills and competencies that their business needs. So, the more skills you get, the better prepared you are for the job market. Other Gallup research shows us that, when hiring, U.S. business leaders say that the amount of knowledge the candidate has in a field, as well as applied skills, are more important factors then where a candidate attended school or what his or her college major was. So, it is the skills portfolio not the degree by itself that really matters.

Transferable skills are particularly important for career success. Transferable skills are those skills that are not job specific and can be used in various settings. They include communication skills, problem solving, teamwork, cross cultural skills, and other skills. A common problem with transferable skills is that there is a huge mismatch between job applicants' perceptions of their readiness for the job and prospective employers' expectations. A topic recently researched by the Association of American Colleges and Universities, AACU, shows that the students' and employers' perceptions of the students' mastery in performing some critically important transferable skills are dramatically different [3]. For example, in regard to written communication skills, 65% of the students tend to think that they are well prepared, whereas only 27% of the employers think the same. In other words, three out of four employers think that students' skills are not marketable.

Based on the above analysis, we have come up with a list of problems that you, as CEO of EnterpriseYou, will need to address to achieve a competitive edge on your area of interest. Are your skills sufficient to fulfill your career plans? What skills should you have in your portfolio? Can you objectively evaluate the current market value of your skills portfolio? How can you demonstrate your actual mastery and marketability of skills? Do your skills solve prospective employer's problem?

An ability to address the aforementioned problems will help you position yourself as a skilled professional, a kind of black belt in the area of your interest. This can be potentially your competitive advantage in the job market whereas it is increasingly difficult to sell to prospective employers one's experiences and credentials. But even if you know exactly what you should include in your skills portfolio and what the level of mastery that you are supposed to achieve in performing those skills is, there is still one more skill that you have to develop. That is the skill of acquiring other skills, also known as self-directed learning. Developing this master skill, a skill to get skilled, is critical for career success.

Overall, in Course 1, you will achieve the following learning and developmental goals. You will embrace the role of the CEO of EnterpriseYou to become responsible for your strategic career self-management, develop a skill based view of yourself, create and begin using career development and skill building tools, such as self-management information system in the career development lab. During weeks two and three, you'll gain knowledge and analytical skills for career self-management. In particular, you will learn how to analyze competencies and skills, develop your skills portfolio and conduct a self-audit of your career development skills, increase self-awareness, and engage in designing your future work self, acquire necessary knowledge and skills for self-strategy and self-direction. During weeks four and five, you'll learn how to apply career self-management skills for professional growth. In particular, you will learn how to develop an objective external view of your skills portfolio, understand competitive selection based on evaluation of candidates' skills portfolios, master evidence-based, data-driven evaluation of required skills, find out how to assess the current market value of your skills portfolio.

In the end of each week we'll invite you to the Career Development Lab, or CDL. CDL is a challenging intellectual gym designed to strengthen your career muscle through weekly workouts. Every workout will begin with a brief video lecture and continue with working on a capstone task. We recommend that you do the workouts sequentially, but you can also skip some and then return later. We hope you will enjoy the course and find it useful for your career development. Welcome to the course!

Works cited:

[1] Shaffer, L.S., & Zalewski, J.M. (2011). Career advising in a VUCA Environment. *NACADA Journal,* 31(1), Spring, pp. 64-74.

[2] 2013 Gallup-Lumina Foundation Business Poll on Higher Education. Gallup, 2013.

[3] AACU Poll on Employer's Perceptions of Graduate Readiness. *Inside Higher Education*, January 20, 2015.

Professional (Skilled) Self

As a human being, you have a multitude of characteristics including your values, abilities, attitudes, aptitudes, etc. In practical terms, when you consider applying for a job, you typically focus on your job-related skills and habits. This is your work identity. In this course, we will call it *Professional (or Skilled) Self.* A professional self is a combination of skills. Let's see how we can characterize skills and how they are developed.

Professional and Generic (= Transferable) Skills

Job-related skills are composed of professional and generic skills. Sometimes, it is difficult to tell whether a certain skill is professional or generic (i.e., not discipline specific). Professional skills are discipline (like marketing research) and even employer specific (for example, mastery of particular software, standards, customer base, etc.); they are transferable within a company or between similar positions in different companies. A certain skill is generic if it is transferable to areas outside a particular position, company or even industry. Generic skills typically include information management, communication, interpersonal, cross-cultural, analytical and problem solving, and self-management skills.

College teaching and skills acquisition

College teaching, particularly in liberal arts and sciences colleges, is mostly concerned with knowledge acquisition in general education, as well as professional areas, and developing foundational generic skills, such as academic writing, information literacy and critical thinking skills, under an assumption that it is the workplace where applied professional and advanced generic skills can and should be developed. As mentioned earlier, there is a certain gap between college teaching and workplace expectations. To help students prepare for the job market, many institutions develop career resources and skill-building courses. An example of a career center is provided by Excelsior College in New York, a skill builder and capability profiler is developed by Griffith University in Australia, a standing alone skill-building course in UK is described by Geoff Baker and Debra Henson in their article "Promoting employability skills development in a research intensive university" (*Education+Training*, 2010, vol. 52(1), pp. 62-75).

To increase job readiness of their graduates, some colleges currently experiment with so called "competency-based" education and assessment; a very interesting example is presented in an article written by Elaine Danneler "The Portfolio approach to competency-based assessment at the Cleveland Clinic Lerner College of Medicine" (*Academic Medicine*, Vol. 82(5), May, 2007, pp. 493-502). The idea behind competency-based education is to build the entire curriculum around assessable skills and competencies, but it appears that it is very difficult to implement this idea in an academic setting. In fact, employability skills are typically the result of many academic and training courses, as well as work-based learning and individual efforts undertaken by students.

Ultimately, it is the students who are the most interested in and responsible for the development of graduate outcomes, including graduate employability skills.

College graduate attributes

With increasing competition in higher education, nationally and globally, many universities around the globe have recognized the need for their graduates to successfully compete on the job market by demonstrating superior graduate employability skills. As a result, those universities have begun emphasizing programs that foster skill-based outcomes ("attributes"). For example, a Griffith University's list of graduate attributes includes professional skills in the disciplines, as well as generic skills, such as communication skills, innovation, social responsiveness and cross-cultural competence. Those skills are mapped by faculty and administrators and linked to courses throughout the curriculum. Some universities (for example, the University of Glasgow in Scotland) have begun promoting self-management, lifelong and self-directed learning skills as desired graduate attributes, as it has become clear that in most occupations it now takes less than a decade for the knowledge base to become obsolete and students should be able to re-educate themselves. You can read more about graduate attributes in the article by Ruth Bridgestock (in the next chapter).

Career development, individual learning goals and career self-management

It is likely that after completing a pre-designed program of studies built around graduate attributes students are better prepared for a reality check on the job market. But what actually happens when all classes are over and there seems to be no way for a worker to secure continuing professional growth and career development other than through self-improvement? It is logical to suggest that at some stage everyone has to learn about how to become her/his own trainer, assessor, and mentor and assume the responsibility for developing career management skills. This is where self-management skills and techniques can be very helpful.

Further readings on career development learning

- Greenhaus, J.H., Callahan, G.A., & Godshalk, V.M. (2010). *Career Management.* 4th ed. Thousand Oaks, CA: SAGE.
- Inkson, K., Dries, N., & Arnold, J. (2015). *Understanding Careers.* 2nd ed. Thousand Oaks, CA: SAGE.
- Watts, A. G. (2006*). Career Development Learning and Employability*. Heslington, York: The Higher Education Academy.

Career Self-Management (Career Building) Skills

Career development, individual learning goals, and career self-management

It is likely that after completing a pre-designed program of studies built around graduate attributes students are better prepared for a reality check on the job market. But what actually happens when all classes are over and there seems to be no way for a worker to secure continuing professional growth and career development other than through self-improvement? It is logical to suggest that at some stage everyone has to learn about how to become her/his own trainer, assessor, and mentor and assume the responsibility for developing career management skills. This is where career self-management skills and techniques can be very helpful.

Career Self-Management: a meta-skill and a strategy for self-development

From a narrow point of view, self-management is concerned with developing personal attributes, motivations, dispositions for a better self-control, and as such it is one of employability skills (DEST, 2002). In a career development perspective, career self-management is an overarching skill of self-observation, self-analysis and self-programming that is needed for any individual striving to accomplish personal and career development goals in a complex environment by mastering a range of professional and generic skills. In other words, self-management is a "meta-skill" (*meta* means "beyond"), i.e., a skill that is needed to develop other skills. Also, it is a strategic skill, because when functioning in a complex, competitive environment, an individual needs to strategically approach their self-development to be acutely aware of the external requirements, to make sure that their goals are realistic, self-analysis is accurate, and self-programming is adequate to reach the goals. In this course, we'll be using a broad definition of "career self-management" as both a meta-skill and a strategy for acquisition of desired employability skills.

In the literature, career self-management is often used interchangeably with "career competencies", "career management", and "career-building skills". There is an excellent article by Ruth Bridgestock that we highly recommend you read:

- Bridgestock, R. (2009). "The graduate attributes we've overlooked: enhancing graduate employability through career management skills". *Higher Education Research and Development*, 28(1), pp. 31-44. Available online at: https://undergrad.ucf.edu/whatsnext/wp-content/uploads/2016/03/The-Graduate-Attributes-Weve-Overlooked.pdf

Setting up your Career e-Portfolio and Learning Journal Workbook (CPW): The 7-step P.S.A.L.T.E.R. process

Why e-portfolio? What is an e-portfolio?

An evidence-based approach to self-management is concerned with collection of records of one's performance and their systematization, measurement, benchmarking, monitoring, etc. It is virtually impossible to conduct all these activities, organize and present their results without using a special instrument which can be a folder, a shelf, or a piece of software for organizing and storing digital copies. E-portfolio has become a popular tool to serve this purpose. These days e-portfolios are used for assessment, presentations, learning, personal development, etc. For example, Elaine Danneler, Geoff Baker and Debra Henson [6, 7] developed an extensive bibliography and provided examples of how e-portfolios are used in educational settings similar to this course. Also, you may find it useful to review Jon Mueller's authentic assessment toolbox.

The use of Career Self-Management e-Portfolio and Learning Journal Workbook in this course

In this course, we will be using a simplistic version of an e-portfolio in the form of a single Word document. On the course webpage, you can find and download the Career Self-Management E-Portfolio and Learning Journal Workbook (CPW) Template. You will need to enter your personal information, rename the file and save it on your hard drive. It's a good idea to use your name in the file's name, for example *<JoeDoeWorkbook.docx>*. In each Module, there will be a CPW submission task labelled CPW1, CPW2, etc. You'll be asked to continuously work in your Workbook and submit the entire Workbook in each Module. All CPW submissions (in Modules 1-5) are subject to grading; in Module 6 you'll be required to review all entries and submit the Workbook as a final project. Overall, CPW tasks and the final submission contribute 30% to your grade for the course. In some Modules, you'll be asked to use attachments (for example, your resume in Module 1).

The tasks in CPW are designed in accordance with the 7-step P.S.A.L.T.E.R. process for effective career self-management that we developed for this course.

The 7-step P.S.A.L.T.E.R. Process for Effective Career Self-Management

Step 1 (P): Strategic **Planning** for superior skills	Analyze today's skill-based, competitive job market environment and identify your personal needs for effective career self-management; review your current skills portfolio and examine your prerequisite career self-management skills; develop a strategic planning approach to skill-building and career growth; identify and begin examining some of the learning theories that underpin personal growth, such as positive psychology, self-directed learning, active regulation, goal setting, situated and transformational learning.
Step 2 (S): Utilizing business **strategy** tools	Identify and examine strategic management tools and techniques that can be used for crafting successful personal strategies in a competitive, skill-based job market environments; apply management and marketing approaches for scanning competitive job market environments in your area of interest;

	implement job market simulation technique (competitive selection) to identify and objectively evaluate your job-related skills.
Step 3 (A): **Auditing** and **analyzing** skills	Analyze job-related competencies and skills; utilize performance management methodologies and tools to identify and objectively evaluate your own job-related competencies and skills.
Step 4 (L): Managing your Skills **Lab**	For any job of your interest, develop an ability to identify the required skillset, to quantify your level of skills acquisition against the likely benchmarks, and to objectively estimate your likely total skillset score in a competitive job selection process.
Step 5 (T): **Transforming** your personal brand	Use strategic marketing approach for collecting, organizing, peer-reviewing, and demonstrating evidence of your mastery of skills for successful job search/promotion.
Step 6 (E): **Effective** self-regulation	Synthesize self-management and self-marketing methods and techniques for data-driven self-programming; design quantifiable (SMARTER) skill-building plans; implement effective training interventions (exercises).
Step 7 R: **Review** and **reinforce**	Review your progress and evaluate the results; utilize information technology for self-monitoring; engage in active self-regulation for managing your skills portfolio and maintaining an effective career development workflow.

The optional use of LinkedIn

LinkedIn (www.linkedin.com) is a popular social media tool; also, it can be used as an e-portfolio. We'll discuss the use of LinkedIn for your self-promotion in Module 5, but there is no requirement for you to actually use LinkedIn in this course.

References

- Baker, G., and Henson, D. (2010). "Promoting employability skills development in a research-intensive university". *Education+Training*, 52(1), 62-75. DOI: http://dx.doi.org.library.esc.edu/10.1108/00400911011017681.
- Bridgestock, R. (2009). "The graduate attributes we've overlooked: enhancing graduate employability through career management skills". *Higher Education Research and Development*, 28(1), 31-44. DOI: 10.1080/07294360802444347.
- Danneler, E. (2007). "The Portfolio approach to competency-based assessment at the Cleveland Clinic Lerner College of Medicine". *Academic Medicine, 82(5),* 493-502.

- DEST (2002). *Employability skills for the future: A report by the Australian Chamber of Commerce and Industry and the Business Council of Australia for the Department of Education, Science and Training*. Canberra, Australia.

- Finch, D., Nadeau, J., and O'Reilly, N. The Future of Marketing Education: A Practitioner's Perspective. *Journal of Marketing Education. 2013, 35(1)*, 54-67. DOI: 10.1177/0273475312465091.

- Jackson, D. (2009). An international profile of industry-relevant competencies and skill gaps in modern graduates. *International Journal of Management Education*, 8(3), 29-58. DOI:10.3794/jime.83.288.

- Jackson, D. (2012). Business undergraduates' perceptions of their capabilities in employability skills: Implications for industry and higher education. *Industry and Higher Education, 26(5),* 345-356. **DOI:** 10.5367/ihe.2012.0117.

- Mueller, J. *The Authentic Assessment Toolbox*. Available at: http://jfmueller.faculty.noctrl.edu/toolbox/portfolios.htm.

Discussion D1: Employability, skills, and careers in the 21st century

Why do employers increasingly focus on the skills that job applicants (should) possess? What are the skills they are typically looking for? Are those skills taught at school or acquired through work? Who is responsible for skills acquisition: Students? Professors? Trainers? Employers? Do people generally need to know more about skills, how to gain them, how to evaluate mastery of skills, how to let employers know about your skills?

Before responding, review the relevant chapters of the textbook, Coursera videos, and the following website: http://www.onetonline.org/

Exercise: Your Skilled-Based Career Growth Matrix

The Matrix consists of four quadrants that represent four different career development scenarios (See Fig.1). The scenarios are "Job Excellence", "Job Enhancement", "Job Diversification", and "Career Change". In the Workbook, we will ask you to identify four scenarios for your skill-based career growth.

Job Diversification Diversifying the Existing Skillset	Career Change Building a Brand New Skillset
Job Excellence Perfecting the Existing Skillset	Job Enhancement Extending the Existing Skillset

Figure 1. The Individual Skills Management Matrix

The model is based on the Ansoff matrix [2] that is commonly used in business strategy as a structured approach to strategy formulation. According to the model, a company has four basic options for strategy development which include: a) using the existing product portfolio to deeper penetrate in the existing markets; b) modernizing the portfolio for the same markets; c) using the old portfolio in the new market; d) using a modernized portfolio in the new markets. Career coaches use a very similar logic when explaining potential scenarios for skill-building.

In our model, scenario "Job Excellence" is to capture a situation where you are interested in strengthening your standing in the current job or obtaining a similar position with another employer. In such a case your job-specific skillset is well-defined and is not going to change, at least in the short run. In this scenario, your plan of actions will include running a skillset check for this job, updating your competency dashboard, reviewing competitive strengths and competency gaps, and developing an evidence-based and data-driven plan for improvement.

The next scenario, "Job Enhancement", takes place when you add a new skill to your existing skillset to secure your current job, or get a promotion, or obtain a similar job with a broader range of responsibilities in another organization. Before you can execute a plan of actions like in the previous scenario, you'll have to learn how to operationalize a skill that you have not mastered yet.

By the way, if there is any sacred knowledge in individual skills management, this is exactly where it is. If you have not yet mastered the skill, how would you possibly know about critical tasks, benchmarks, and the required level of proficiency? Well, this is one of the main topics to explore in the following Modules.

Yet another career development scenario is called "Job Diversification". This scenario is to capture a situation when you are planning to master a new skill from another vocational field. For example, you are in Marketing and you are thinking of taking on Finance or Business Analytics. Technically, this scenario is similar to "Job Enhancement", but it may be much harder to do in the unknown area.

Finally, scenario "Career Change" represents a situation where you will need to design and build a completely new skillset. It may seem to be hard, but the idea is that the more often you do it, the easier it gets.

This exercise is adopted from: Chukhlomin, V. (2018). *How to Get Skilled.* Upward Mobility Books, Saratoga Springs, NY.

Works cited:

[1] Ansoff, H. Igor (1979). Corporate Strategy. Hammondworth, Eng.: Penguin Books.

Module M2:

Individual Skills Management

Overview

This course is developed with business students in mind who can build on their management and marketing knowledge and skills for developing and executing a sound personal strategy. The overarching goal of this Module is to help you utilize a business strategy approach to effectively self-manage your skills portfolio.

In this Module, we examine strategic management tools and techniques, such as SWOT analysis and Competitive Analysis, for guiding career development activities in competitive job market environments. Similar to strategic planners in the corporate world who use SWOT analysis to develop the company's key competencies and to eventually achieve a competitive advantage, strategically oriented career builders can utilize business strategy for achieving a competitive edge in the skill-based job market environment. To do so, you will initially engage in a conversation about the applicability of the SWOT analysis for career growth. Then, as a practical application, we will ask you to engage in a realistic simulation of a competitive job selection process in your area of expertise/interest. First, acting as an employer, you will prepare a set of skill-based selection criteria for a given position. Then, acting as a prospective employee, you will address the selection criteria and prepare a detailed selection criteria statement. After that, in Module 3, we will ask you to switch back to the employer's role, thoroughly examine and evaluate your selection criteria statement, and discuss the findings with your peers.

A thorough, meticulous, objective, and honest self-analysis is the foundation of career self-management. In order to strategically plan and perform self-developmental activities individuals must develop specific metacognitive and self-regulatory skills and motivational beliefs. When empowered with those skills and beliefs, individuals become self-directed, strategically oriented and more efficient in performing various activities, such as education (self-directed learners) and work (goal-oriented employees). In the Module, we examine the specifics of self-analysis in a competitive business environment. In particular, we'll see that in a competitive job market where individuals compete for jobs/promotions and are routinely benchmarked against standards, best practices and each other's performances, it is critically important for an employee/job seeker to develop an objective, external view of their own competencies and skills. Taking an external perspective is helpful for conducting an objective, evidence-based self-assessment, correctly interpreting its results by comparing and rating them against standards or the competition, and then developing sound strategies for self-promotion and self-development. In the Module, we begin examining various analytical methods and tools including benchmarking that were originally developed by business strategists for organizations striving to achieve competitive advantage and discuss whether and how some of those methods and tools can be used by individuals aiming to succeed in a competitive job market.

Module Learning Objectives:

M2-1	Identify methods and techniques originally developed for business strategy in the corporate environment that can be used for planning a sound personal strategy in a competitive job market environment.	**R2, D2**
M2-2	Identify your generic, professional, and personal skills.	**CPW2**
M2-3	Apply SWOT Analysis for analyzing your job-related skills and discuss your findings with the peers.	**CPW2, D2**
M2-4	Working in a simulated workplace environment, identify a required skillset and develop corresponding selection criteria for prospective candidates.	**A2-1**
M2-5	Responding to the selection criteria, prepare a mock selection criteria statement.	**A2-2**

VIDEO LECTURE: Managing Oneself as a Business

This video filmed for "Career Brand Management" specialization in 2016 compares managing one's personal development with running a business enterprise and dives deeper into business strategy seeking to find important knowledge for individual career builders.

Please note that in this and other videos we refer to courses in the Coursera's Career Brand Management specialization. The specialization follows the same logic as this course, though the sequence of activities is slightly different.

Hello again! In previous presentations, we discussed the advantages of having a tool that would allow you to measure the effectiveness of skill building activities.

Before we continue exploring skill building in more detail, let's think about this activity in the context of overall self-strategy. This is important because business strategy tools, such as a SWOT analysis, are very popular and widely used for career advising. But the problem is that those tools are often misunderstood and misused. So, let's talk about what we can learn from business strategy.

To begin, let's review how we dealt with strategic issues in Course 1. You may recall that we quoted Peter Drucker, the father of contemporary management, who wrote that each knowledge worker must think and behave as a Chief Executive Officer [1]. What does that mean exactly? In the corporate environment, a CEO is the senior decision maker who is ultimately responsible for the company's performance and its strategic direction. So, it is the full responsibility that a career developer must embrace, the strategic function that he or she must perform, which makes his or her situation similar to one of being a CEO of a corporation.

Following Drucker's advice, in Course 1, we implemented the concept of strategic planning to personal development and came up with the notion of self-strategy. Then we identified and explored the elements of self-strategy including self-observation, self-awareness, personal mission and values, self-regulated behaviors, scanning the job market environment, long term and immediate goal setting, envisioning one's future work self and engaging in self-directed learning. All of that is helpful for self-development as it provides a big picture view of one's career development and focuses on long term goals. But how can we get even more from business strategy? For example, can we use business strategy methods and techniques for guiding, organizing, and monitoring skill building activities?

Take, for example, SWOT analysis. It is rare to find a career development resource that doesn't mention the need for the learner to conduct a SWOT analysis. One may think that the tool is so simple and so powerful that anyone can easily master and create a sound career strategy. The truth is the tool was not developed for career advising or personal development. It belongs to field of corporate strategy and even in its native environment, it doesn't have any analytical capacity on its own. In other words, while using SWOT analysis may look cool and scientific, in reality it can be useless and even misleading. As they say in information technology, garbage in, garbage out.

You may recall this chart from Course 1. It is showing differences in perceptions of work readiness by recent graduates and prospective employers. According to the American Association of Colleges and Universities research, 65% of graduates think that their communication skills are strong, but only 27% of employers agree [2]. In other words, the very same competency that is seen by many graduates as their strength, is in the eyes of their employers a weakness. So, if someone attempted to conduct a SWOT analysis of his or her skills, based solely on a gut feeling, he or she would probably come up with a very inaccurate and misleading conclusion about their strengths and weaknesses, which in turn may disorient the person in his or her career decisions. As a result, a good job opportunity may be lost.

Meanwhile, there are good jobs available. But employers cannot fill them because of the mismatch between job requirements and candidates' skills. According to Tara Sinclair, Chief Economist to indeed.com, 38% of employers report difficulties filling jobs [3]. One quarter of jobs in the U.S. are made open after 60 days and close to 5 million jobs are unfilled. The conclusion is that existing methods of work force development, career advising, and self-improvement may not be providing job seekers with adequate guidance and sufficient preparation. Using sophisticated techniques like a SWOT analysis is not going to help either unless those tools are properly use. To understand how a SWOT analysis actually works, it's good to become familiar with the relevant literature or to take a course on business strategy.

You maybe surprise to learn that according to researchers Chermack and Kasshanna [4], and many others, there are many misconceptions about the use of a SWOT analysis even in the field of corporate strategy where it belongs. For valid results, business analysts need to undertake some preparation and a lot of preliminary work. Why do you think that using a SWOT analysis is easier in the field of career development?

This question brings us to the point where we should ask ourselves whether an analytical tool rooted in business strategy can be applied for career development. Or, in general terms, can we draw on business strategy to derive conclusions and obtain tools that are applicable for individual career strategy? Metaphors and analogies can help us navigate new areas and grasp new concepts by comparing the unknown and what we already know. Here's an example of a popular business metaphor. Chess is a strategy game. So, it is rare to find a book or course on strategy without an image of chess pieces on the cover. It does not mean that the business strategists, academics, and business students are supposed to play chess and learn strategy from that. Typically, they do not. So, chess playing methods and techniques like the Sicilian defense are useless in the context of business strategy. The strategist still seem to like using chess pieces for decorating their books. Probably because using chess pieces images remind them of the need to be thoughtful, wise, competitive and of course strategic.

To answer this question, we need to focus on similarities between a firm's behavior, competitive markets of goods and services, and individual behavior in competitive job markets. Fortunately, there are many good courses on business strategy, including those on Coursera that can help. When studying business strategy, we recommend that you pay particular attention to a theory suggested by Barney in 1991 and called "The Resource-Based View of the Firm" [5]. According to this theory, the key for the sustainable competitive advantage, the firm is in its ability to possess unique resources and develop superior capabilities over the competitors. The theory provides a blueprint for strategic analysis, which includes the following steps. Analyzing the attractiveness of the industry, identifying key success factors for the industry, evaluating the firm's resources and capabilities, conducting benchmarking against competitors and identifying the firms core competencies and generating strategies for gaining the competitive advantage. In a nutshell, the theory recommends that a company striving for a competitive edge must position itself in an industry where it has natural advantages, then identify key requirements for success in that industry. Compare the resources and capabilities with the competition. Analyze the results and develop and implement a winning strategy.

There is a certain similarity between "The Resource-Based View of the Firm," and the skill-based view of the individual. As "The Resource-Based View of the Firm" is a well-established theory and methodology of analysis in the business world, it is safe to suggest that when dealing with the skill based view of the individual on a competitive job market, one can draw on the ideas and tools commonly used by business strategists. As a result of this exercise, we will have a blueprint for strategic planning in the field of individual career development. In Course 1, we already conducted some of the necessary steps. Including developing a skill-based view of yourself and identifying critically important skills in the area of your interest. In Course 2, we will pay particular attention to benchmarking for assessment and self-assessment. Benchmarking is a critically important step because it reveals true strengths and weaknesses or competency gaps. Only after that, you will have enough materials to conduct a meaningful SWOT analysis and craft a realistic personal career development plan.

Let's summarize our findings. One of the most important takeaways from business strategy is that a meaningful SWOT analysis can only be done after benchmarking the company's resources and capabilities against their competitors and revealing the firm's true strengths and weaknesses. The same logic seems to hold true for career development. It does not make much sense to ask someone about his or her strengths before running benchmarking tests. As we demonstrated earlier, self-assessments based on a gut feeling are proven to be inaccurate and misleading. It is critically important to learn how to make them realistic. A failure to conduct an accurate self-assessment prevents individuals from detecting and addressing competency gaps. Gaps in turn prevent individuals from landing good jobs. And remember, there are millions of jobs available in the US. Do not allow your competency gaps to slow down your career. On a positive side, a properly conducted self-assessment will help detect and eliminate competency gaps. That's all for today, see you in the career development lab."

Works cited:

[1] Drucker, P. (2005). Managing Oneself. *Harvard Business Review*, January.

[2] AACU Poll on Employer's Perceptions of Graduate Readiness. *Inside Higher Education*, January 20, 2015.

[3] Sinclair, T. Labor Market Outlook 2016: Uncovering the Causes of Global Jobs Mismatch. Indeed.com.

[4] Chermack, T.J., & Kasshanna, B.K.(2007). The Use and Misuse of SWOT Analysis and Implications for HRD Professionals. *Human Resource Development International*, 10 (4), pp. 383-399.

[5] Barney, J.B. (1991). Is the Resource-Based Theory a Useful Perspective for Strategic Management Research? Yes. *Academy of Management Review*, 26(1), pp. 41-56.

Learning from business strategy

Why do you need to take an external view of your skill base?

In this Module, we begin by examining the specifics of self-strategy in a business context. Then, we will describe a model of strategic self-management as the cornerstone of career self-management in a competitive business environment.

In a competitive job market environment, individuals compete for jobs/promotions and are routinely benchmarked against standards, best practices, and each other's performances. If someone wants to learn a particular skill to increase their employability, this individual must develop a fairly good idea about the required level of performance to withstand the competition.

Therefore, when conducting self-analysis in a business context, an individual must be aware of desired skills/levels of competency, their factual skills/levels of competence and develop an objective, external view of their own performance. Taking an external perspective is helpful for conducting an objective, evidence-based self-analysis and self-assessment, correctly interpreting its results by comparing and rating them against standards or the competition, and then developing sound strategies for self-development.

Benchmarking

Benchmarking is the key component of self-analysis in a business context; to find out about true strengths and weaknesses in someone's' skill repertoire, it should be compared and matched with the competition. Contemporary learning theories are not concerned with this problem; not surprisingly that the training and development literature dealing with self-developmental issues must often "borrow" ideas, concepts, and approaches from the business strategy literature where the concept of competitive benchmarking was born. That's how "personal SWOT", "personal balanced scoring card" and the like models have been introduced for developmental purposes.

In this module we review analytical methods and tools including benchmarking that were originally developed by business strategists for organizations striving to achieve competitive advantage and discuss whether and how some of those methods and tools can be used by individuals aiming to succeed in a competitive job market. To begin with, we review main ideas of business strategy and discuss whether and if yes then how it can be used for strategic career self-management.

A "crash" course on strategy

It is likely that as a business student you are already familiar with the concept of business strategy and have mastered some tools of strategic planning. In preparation for this Module's activities, you may find it useful to browse your old textbooks or google <business strategy> and review search results. To make sure that we are on the same page, we would like to take a minute and improvise a "crash course" on strategy.

In its simplest definition, **strategy** is about going from here to there where "here" is the current and "there" a desired situation in a competitive and ever-changing environment. Strategic approach typically requires a strategist to begin with conducting an analysis where s/he would identify values and goals of the organization and its main stakeholders, then analyses external and internal environments and future trends, conducts internal analysis and benchmarks the organization against its competition, examines the current and formulates a range of possible future strategies, recommends one of those and suggests implementation steps and control strategies. In ancient times, strategic approach was widely used by military and political leaders; in the modern era strategy was re-invented and is commonly used by large corporations, non-profit and governmental bodies and even small businesses. Strategic models and tools can also be used by individuals.

Developing business strategy is not a science, but a way of disciplined thinking; as such, it is helpful for analyzing the environment, identifying available choices, developing a logical course of actions. As a result, strategic thinking may yield significant benefits. It is believed that if a business, organization or an individual has done the analytical part right and is capable of pursuing a coordinated course of actions, chances are that it will indeed be possible to get from "here" to "there" or at least very close. But how can an individual engage in strategic planning? Are there any rules or "scientific" recommendations?

Of course, there are no "magic" tools and the fact that someone uses "scientific" methods like SWOT analysis provides no guarantee. When conducting strategic analysis, it is important to understand its logic and the way business strategists use their instruments to obtain meaningful results. Having said that, let's examine what some of the popular concepts/instruments of strategic analysis are and how they can be used for self-analysis.

Strategy: In the beginning, it should be very clearly and explicitly stated where you are going from and where you want to be.

Mission/vision: This is a very crucial point for strategic analysis. For a company, typical questions are: Who are we? What business are we in? What do we want to be? In 1 year? In 5 years from now? Similar questions should be asked by an individual conducting strategic self-analysis.

Stakeholders: Who are significant others? What is their influence? How might this affect your plans? There are specific tools to analyze stakeholders and their influence, but it's probably better not to dig too deep at this stage.

External scanning: What is the external environment and its boundaries? What is happening in the environment politically? Economically? Socially? Culturally? Technologically? Why does (or doesn't) it matter in your case? What opportunities and threats are present in the external environment? Today and in near future?

Competitive environment: What is the immediate competition in attaining your goal(s)? What are the key success factors typically shared by successful competitors and apparently required in this particular environment to succeed? What else is happening in this industry (occupation, location)? Short term and long-term trends? What opportunities and threats are in the internal (competitive) environment?

Internal analysis and benchmarking: What are your capabilities, attitudes and dispositions, competencies and skills? Are your knowledge base and preparation sufficient? What are your chances to succeed in the competitive environment, now and in the future?

Summary: Strategic summary combines the results of external and internal analyses and provides a foundation for strategy formulation.

Strategy formulation begins with identification and evaluation of alternatives. Oftentimes it requires **making assumptions** about changes in the environment and competitive moves and re-evaluating previous analyses. Strategy making is not a one-time process!

Once the overall strategy is formulated and translated into a series of steps and **functional strategies**, it should be consistently **implemented, monitored and controlled**.

Strategic tools

There are many strategic models that are commonly used to conduct analyses and present findings. One of the most popular is SWOT (Strengths, Weaknesses, Opportunities, Threats) Analysis.

SWOT is a model (=strategic tool) to present a summary of findings where Opportunities and Threats identified by scanning external and internal environments are matched against internal Weaknesses and Strengths. This tool is developed to summarize findings of strategic analysis, evaluate current and formulate new strategies. SWOT is a popular tool that is often used, but also commonly misunderstood. To properly use SWOT analysis, one needs to meticulously conduct all required analytical procedures.

A typical mistake, for example, is to start working on strategic analysis by doing SWOT. Without developing a reasonably good understanding of the environment and ongoing trends it is very easy to miscalculate opportunities, threats, strengths and weaknesses. Let's consider a hypothetical situation where someone is an exceptionally good typist and sees it as a major strength to build a job search strategy. This person might be upset to find out that due to advances in speech recognition technology typing speed may no longer be seen by employers as an advantage.

Another typical mistake is to mix up an external threat and an internal weakness ("my weakness is that my skill has no value anymore"). You cannot change the environment; it is beyond your control, so some changes in the external environment can present a threat if you are not prepared to change internally. The question is whether you can see that your real weakness is perhaps your inability to scan the environment and change. If you engage in scanning the environment and will be looking for ways to adapt and succeed, it is likely that you will soon identify a new set of skills to develop and won't be concentrating on your outdated skill.

Another, less known tool is called VRINE (Valuable, Rare, Inimitable, Non-substitutable, Exploitable) and designed for benchmarking resources and capabilities of competing firms.

Using business strategy for personal development

In organizations, some people (like CEO) do strategic planning on a full-time basis; this is their job. Is there any sense for an average person to engage in strategic self-planning? Even if the answer is affirmative, does personal strategy making need to be that elaborated and multistage as the corporate one? Are there any shortcuts? Actually, this is a very interesting question and we would like to leave it for discussion D2. To begin with, you may google <personal SWOT analysis>.

CAISSA: gaining a competitive edge in a skill-based job selection

From business strategy to personal strategy

Building on the advances in cognitive psychology (see more in the next Module), one may conclude that self-management is based upon metacognitive, self-regulatory and motivational processes that allow individuals to develop capabilities for self-observation, self-awareness, self-analysis, goal setting, self-programming, self-monitoring and self-directing. Self-regulatory techniques and approaches include self-observation, self-reflection, self-monitoring and journaling, self-analysis and self-assessment, feedback and support seeking, and strategic, long term orientation. When functioning in a business context and using self-management for achieving competitive advantage on the job market, an individual must be acutely aware of the required skills/levels of competence, set their learning goals accordingly, develop an objective, external view of their own performance, and establish an effective process for strategic self-analysis and self-assessment based on benchmarking of their performance against relevant standards, best practices in the field, or the competition. While psychological theories help us better understand the foundations and internal mechanics of self-management, we need specific, operational approaches and tools for implementing self-management in a business-like, competitive job market context. Some of the approaches and tools that can be borrowed from strategic management include strategic analysis of external environments, identification of key success factors, competitive benchmarking, and SWOT analysis.

CAISSA

As stated earlier, the innovative approach we have developed for this course is called the Contextual Advancement of Individual Skills for Sustainable Competitive Advantage (CAISSA). Drawing on the models and tools derived from business strategy (like SWOT analysis, VRIO, Competitive Analysis), we are asking you to imagine what it would be like if you were a C.E.O. of EnterpriseYOU charged with designing and implementing a winning personal strategy to gain a competitive edge in a skill-based, job competition. In this Module, you examine strategic management tools and techniques, such as SWOT analysis and competitive analysis, for guiding career development activities in competitive job market environments. Similar to strategic planners in the corporate world who use SWOT analysis to develop the company's key competencies and to eventually achieve a competitive advantage, strategically oriented career builders can utilize business strategy for achieving a competitive edge in the skill-based job market environment. As a practical application, we will ask you to engage in a realistic simulation of a competitive job selection process in your area of expertise/interest.

A personal career development lab

To efficiently use the described above method, one needs to engage in collecting evidence of own performance in the critical skills areas, gathering artifacts of best practices and standards in the specified skills areas, selecting tools for self-assessment, conducting self-assessment by benchmarking their performance against standards or competition, and organizing and making sense of findings. This is what we called a personal, career development lab.

Next steps explained (Assignment 2 and beyond)

All students participating in this course are uniquely positioned in their external environment; therefore, critical skills areas for positions (jobs) they may want to get are different. Particularly, required professional skills can be very distinctive. In order to be on the same page with the entire class, we recommend that you focus on generic, transferrable skills. In Assignment 2 students are required to conduct an analysis of their respective external environments and come up with a description for a real of fictitious position of interest. Most importantly, students have to describe key selection criteria for potential candidates for this position emphasizing required competencies and skills for that position. This is a very important assignment as each student will be constantly referring to the selection criteria they specified for the duration of the course.

It is up to students how they approach external analysis; each industry, region or company is unique. Also, students may choose to think about a position that is in close proximity or "think big" about a dream job. It may be helpful to use business strategy tools like PEST analysis to identify future trends and prospects for each occupation or use the Occupational Outlook Handbook published by the U.S. Department of Labor.

Once you will have identified critical skills areas and performance indicators (key success factors for competitive advantage in the chosen field), you'll be ready to engage in internal (self) analysis and self-assessment which is the subject matter of the next two modules.

Responding to Selection Criteria

As a practical application, we ask you to engage in a realistic simulation of a competitive job selection process in your area of expertise/interest. First, acting as an employer, you will prepare a set of skill-based selection criteria for a given position. Then, acting as a prospective employee, you will address the selection criteria and prepare a detailed selection criteria statement. After that, you will switch back to the employer's role, thoroughly examine and evaluate the resultant selection criteria statement, and discuss it with your peers.

To read more about selection criteria, you may use google search. Please note that employers in the U.S. do not necessarily require prospective applicants to respond to the selection criteria by preparing a document titled "Selection Criteria Statement" (though, in other countries this is a well-established practice). Instead, answers to the selection criteria are often included in a covering letter or solicited during an interview. Also, below are some good sources of information:

- Highhouse, S., Doverspike, D., & Guion, R. (2016). *Essentials of Personnel Assessment and Selection.* 2nd ed. Routledge: New York.
- Villiers, A. (2005). *How to Write and Talk to Selection Criteria: Improving Your Chances of Wining a Job.* 4th ed. Mental Nutrition: ACT, Australia.

Self-awareness

Engaging in self-observation and developing self-awareness is the first step of effective career self-management. In any large book store, as well as online, you can find many scholarly, as well as popular, "know thyself" type of sources dealing with problems of understanding of the self and others, explaining and exploring topics like human life cycles, body and wellness, mind and mind power, thinking skills and creativity, behavior styles, spirit and self-esteem, values and interests, lifelong learning, work and life balance, and personal life strategies. As a short cut, you may find it useful to conduct a brief google search and get familiar with the concept of self-awareness.

If you are interested to learn more about how "knowing thyself" translates into job readiness, you may find it useful to conduct a personality assessment test using the Holland's hexagon model (*Note*: The tool is provided by a third party. The college doesn't have any control over it and cannot validate it. Please read carefully their disclaimer and decide whether you want to use it to conduct the test. Alternatively, you can read about the test in the literature). A renowned career theorist, Holland developed a model of six personality types (Realistic, Conventional, Enterprising, Social, Artistic, and Investigative) where typical careers match certain personality types. These days many career centers use this model to help students find out about their personality type and possible careers/occupations they are supposed to be leaning to according to Holland.

A brief resource guide on talent management and strength finders

Sometimes people are not very much interested in knowing more about themselves as employees, but their employers typically do want to know more about ways to increase productivity of their human capital. A selection of employee testing tools can be found on the Pan's Powered website (www.panpowered.com). Using this search tool, you can find companies specializing in development of assessment and self-assessment tools for employers and learn about their products. For example, "My Thinking Styles" assessment developed by Judy Chartrand for THINK Watson is administered by Pearson (a sample report is freely available online). According to the author, identifying a person's thinking style can help the person become more aware of how she/he approaches problems and opportunities, evaluates information, makes decisions, and takes actions. As a result, the person is supposed to become more aware of her/his strengths and how to use them on the job. Another popular tool for finding personal strengths is offered by Gallup (StrengthsFinder). Yet another set of assessment tools is developed by TalentLens (talentlens.com). On their website you can find sample reports demonstrating how they approach skills assessment, the range of assessable skills and the way achieved scores are interpreted.

On individual differences and learning styles

When conducting self-analysis, it's helpful to know about one's thinking and learning styles. The concepts of styles ("thinking style", "learning style") are widely used by psychologists to capture individual differences and explain how people within categories think, learn and approach problems. If this is something that truly interests you, you may want it useful to take at some point a formal class in educational psychology or read a textbook on that subject. For the purpose of this class, we recommend that you read excerpts from three articles. When reading, try to identify your own learning style and think about how you can use a better understanding of your personality type when looking for a job.

Mark Morrison, Arthur Sweeney and Troy Heffenan ("Learning Styles of On-Campus and Off-Campus Marketing Students: The Challenge for Marketing Educators", *Journal of Marketing Education*, 2003, 25(3), pp. 208-217) provide a brief introduction to theories of learning styles (pp. 209-210), particularly the one of Solomon-Felder and their Index of Learning Styles that includes four dimensions (active/reflective, visual/verbal, sensing/intuitive and sequential/global). Knowing a person's learning style helps better understand the person's teaching and learning preferences and even job potential (p. 215).

David Ackerman and Jing Hu ("Effect of Type of Curriculum on Educational Outcomes and Motivation among Marketing Students with Different Learning Styles", *Journal of Marketing Education*, 2011, 33(3), pp. 273-284) describe Kolb's Learning Style Inventory, Dunn and Dunn's model of learning style preferences, and use Martinez's model of learning orientation where learning styles can be categorized into four groups: transforming learners, performing learners, conforming learners and resistance learners (pp. 273-275). The authors' conclusion is that autonomous learners benefit from hands-on projects, cases and simulations; less autonomous learners are less willing to take the initiative or responsibility for their learning.

Hulia Julie Yazici ("A study of collaborative learning style and team learning performance. *Education & Training*, 2005, 47(2), pp. 216-229) uses another model, the Grasha-Riechmann Student Learning Style Scale (GRSLSS), to assess the learning style preferences of business students enrolled in an operations management class. GRSLSS measures learning styles as personal qualities that influence a student's ability to acquire information, to interact with peers and the teacher, and otherwise to participate in learning experiences. According to the authors,

> *"The learning styles inventory promotes understanding of learning in a broad context, spanning six categories: competitive, collaborative, avoidant, participant, dependent, and independent. Competitive students learn material in order to perform better than others in the class. Collaborative students feel they can learn by sharing ideas and talents. Avoidant style learners are not enthusiastic about learning content and attending class. Participants are good citizens in class. They are eager to do as much of the required and optional course requirements. Dependent learners show little intellectual curiosity and they learn only what is required. They view teacher and peers as sources of structure and support and look for authority figures. Independent learners like to think for themselves and are confident in their learning abilities: they prefer to learn the content that they feel is important"* (p. 222).

On self-control, self-regulation, metacognition, and motivation

Self-control, or an ability to engage in self-observation, planning, goal setting, organizing, self-monitoring and self-evaluation, is the quintessence of self-management. In recent years, the concept of self-control has been actively researched in its application to the field of education; this research area has become known as self-regulated learning (SRL). To get familiar with its main ideas, we highly recommend you reading an article by Barry Zimmerman on the topic ("Self-regulated learning and academic achievement: an overview". *Educational Psychologist*, 1990, 25(1), pp. 3-17) or a more recent work by Traci Sitzmann and Katherine Ely ("Meta-Analysis of Self-Regulated Learning in Work-Related Training and Educational Attainment: What We Know and Where We Need to Go". *Psychological Bulletin*, 2011, 137 (3), pp. 421–442.

In a nutshell, SRL is about 'learning to learn' and then using this crucial skill for self-improvement. There are several aspects of SRL including metacognition, motivation and behavior. Metacognition deals with understanding of one's thinking and learning processes; it enables self-awareness and manifests in a meaningful and efficient planning, goal setting, and self-monitoring. In terms of motivation, self-regulated learners develop and maintain interest, demonstrate high persistence and self-efficacy. Behaviorally, they create personal learning environments, actively seek feedback and develop capabilities for self-instruction.

Self-directedness and a strategic approach to self-management

Self-directedness is a practical application of self-regulation. Broadly speaking, self-directed are those individuals that take full responsibility for all or most aspects of their life. In a narrow sense, self-directedness applies to learning. Self-directed learning (SDL) is a strategic process where individuals analyze their learning needs, formulate learning goals, identify resources, choose and implement strategies and evaluate learning outcomes. A good introduction to SDL can be found in an article by Andrea Ellinger (The Concept of Self-Directed Learning and Its Implications for Human Resource Development, *Advances in Developing Human Resources,* May 2004, 6(2), pp. 158-177.

The concept of self-directedness is very useful to understand how self-management works. To be self-directed, an individual must learn how to effectively control her/his own self and make sure that daily routines contribute to fulfillment of established goals. A toolbox of required skills includes self-observation, self-analysis, goal setting, perseverance and self-regulation, self-monitoring and self-assessment. To efficiently observe and monitor oneself, one needs to develop reflective skills. This is the heart and soul of career self-management.

Reflection and the role of learning journals

When managing others, a manager needs to establish and maintain a system of records describing the assigned tasks and helping monitor performance. Similarly, self-management is easier when there is a written record of self-observation. A discussion of benefits of reflecting practice and various approaches to journaling can be found here. In this course, we use a single document combining a reflective journal, an e-portfolio, and a career e-portfolio. In the end of the course, we will discuss how you can continue this kind of self-developmental work into the future.

References:

- Morrison, M., Sweeney, A., and Heffenan, T. (2003). "Learning Styles of On-Campus and Off-Campus Marketing Students: The Challenge for Marketing Educators", *Journal of Marketing Education*, 2003, 25(3), 208-217. DOI: 10.1177/0273475303257520.

- Ackerman, D., and Jing Hu (2011). "Effect of Type of Curriculum on Educational Outcomes and Motivation among Marketing Students with Different Learning Styles", *Journal of Marketing Education*, 33(3), 273-284. DOI: 10.1177/0273475311420233.

- Yazici, H. J. (2005). A study of collaborative learning style and team learning performance. *Education & Training*, 47(2), 216-229.

- Sitzmann, T., and Ely, K. (2011). Meta-Analysis of Self-Regulated Learning in Work-Related Training and Educational Attainment: What We Know and Where We Need to Go. *Psychological Bulletin*, 137(3), 421–442.

- Zimmerman, B. J. (1990). "Self-Regulated Learning and Academic Achievement: An Overview". *Educational Psychologist*, 25(1), 3-17. DOI: 10.1207/s15326985ep2501_2.

- Ellinger, A. (2004). The Concept of Self-Directed Learning and Its Implications for Human Resource Development. *Advances in Developing Human Resources, 6(2),* 158-177. DOI: 10.1177/1523422304263327.

Discussion D2: Using business strategy for gaining a competitive edge: A personal SWOT analysis

As a student of business, you may know well that companies use many sophisticated models and techniques (for example, SWOT Analysis) to gain a competitive edge on the market. How can we use those proven methods of strategic analysis for individual career self-management?

Before responding, search the Internet for "personal SWOT Analysis" and review the relevant sections in the course text and – if you subscribed for extra credit - watch Coursera videos. In your main post, share with your classmates a skill-based SWOT (Strengths, Weaknesses, Opportunities, Threats) Analysis of yourself.

Is your SWOT analysis accurate? How do you know that? What does it tell you? Do you think that for different jobs you would come up with different SWOT analysis results? Why so? So what?

Module M3:

Self-Audit and Skills Analysis

Overview

Module 3 is to teach you how to use performance management methods and techniques to analyze and evaluate your job-related skills. In this (and the following) Modules, you will learn how to utilize performance management methodologies, originally developed in the corporate world, for skills assessment and individual skills management.

To accurately measure and monitor the level of skills acquisition in a competitive job market environment, you will first need to examine how you can operationalize skills and quantify the level of skills acquisition so that you can realistically estimate a total skillset score for each job-specific skillset. This was you will be able to estimate and predict your competitive standing in a job contest. Also, you will get a much better idea about your skill-building goals. To do so, we will be using tools and techniques derived from human resource management. Topics in this Module include competency frameworks, units and elements of competency, critical tasks, mastery of performance, benchmarking, skills assessment, expert and peer assessment, and self-assessment. In the end of the Module, you will use Critical Skills Assessment Tool to analyze, and objectively evaluate the level of your mastery in one or several job-related, critical skill areas.

As mentioned earlier, in order to conduct a thorough and objective self-assessment, it is critically important to approach it from an objective, external point of view. That's why we begin by asking you to review your own skills analysis crafted in Module 2 Assignment 2 by looking through the lens of a potential employer in Discussion 3. Then, you will examine the foundations and mechanics of self-assessment drawing from four distinctly different bodies of literature (educational psychology, vocational development and training, graduate employability skills and management science). In particular, you will review self-assessment principles as formulated by educational theorists and practitioners, examine assessment and self-assessment methodologies, frameworks, instruments and tools, examine the use of self-assessment techniques in relation to transition from college to work and the formation of graduate employability skills, observe approaches to collecting, organizing, presenting and evaluating evidence of mastery of skills. You will also examine how business strategists' approach self-assessment in their companies and discuss whether some of the business strategy tools (like VRINE model) or their modifications can be used for personal self-assessment. As a practical application, students will be able to use a special instrument developed for this course ("Critical Skills Assessment Tool"). When working on Written Assignment 3, you will also describe the process of self-assessment and reflect on the suggested readings.

Module Learning Objectives:

M3-1	Examine performance management concepts and methodologies, such as competency frameworks, units and elements of competency, critical tasks, and discuss their applicability for individual skills management.	**R3**

M3-2	Critically review and analyze the selection criteria statement that you created in the previous Module and try to guestimate your likely skillset score in a job competition for the position you specified.	**D3**
M3-3	Identify the critical tasks that can be used for evaluating your mastery of skills for the chosen position.	**CPW3**
M3-4	Review the concept of benchmarking as used in the corporate world and examine its applicability for individual skills management.	**R3, CPW3**
M3-5	Identify benchmarks, assessment methods and tools for skills assessment in the above exercise.	**CPW3**
M3-6	Conduct self-assessment of your skills using the provided Critical Skills Assessment Tool (CSAT).	**A3-1**
M3-7	Examine your findings in light of the relevant competency frameworks and skill assessment methodologies.	**A3-2**

VIDEO LECTURE: How to Operationalize and Measure Skills

This video lecture is taken from "How to Get Skilled", an advanced level Coursera course for working professionals, filmed in 2018. In the lecture, we describe the process of competitive selection.

Please note that in this video we refer to courses on Coursera that follow the same logic as this course, though the sequence of activities is slightly different.

A prominent management thinker, Peter Drucker, once noted "You cannot manage what you cannot measure" [1]. In this lecture, we'll explore a practical approach to measuring job related skills in a competitive job market environment.

To effectively manage job related skills, one needs to find a way to objectively measure her or his current level of skill acquisition, as it relates to a given job. For example, if you are considering applying for a job that has certain skill requirements, would it be helpful for you to know your objective ranking against the ideal candidate on a scale of 1-100? If you possessed an ability to do so. You would be able to see what your current standing on the job market is and how you could improve it. But the problem is that it is easy to say but hard to do. The concept of skill acquisition is fuzzy and very difficult to measure. Before we begin, we shall talk about what exactly we are going to measure and how we are going to do it.

When attempting to measure a fuzzy and elusive concept, like skill acquisition, you need to first operationalize it, in other words, to find a way to pinpoint it and make it measurable. To operationalize skills acquisition, we suggest that you think about skills not in isolation, but in terms of compact job specific skill sets. A skill set is a specific combination of skills that are required for a given job. In most cases, you can interpret the required skill set from a detailed job description. Usually, required skills are mentioned explicitly, but they can also be hiding under job duties, competencies, and certifications. Deriving a required skill set from the corresponding job description, is a fun exercise that we highly recommend you do. You may begin with your current job, or any job that you are familiar with, where you have gained a detailed knowledge of the required skill set. Can you identify the most important skills or key competencies that are vitally important to succeed on the job?

As a result of this exercise, you should be able to come up with a compact list of skills for a given job. Now, after you have learned how to organize your skills into a well-defined job specific skill set, let's talk more about skill sets in general. Skill sets are important because this is exactly what employers and recruiters are looking for. Not one skill, but a specific combination of skills for specific projects. If you want to know more about skill sets that are typically required by U.S. employers, you can read about it in excellent reports published by Burning Glass Technologies, a job market analytics company based in Boston Massachusetts [2]. The company has developed a unique methodology for analyzing demand for skilled workforce by sectors, and what is important for this course, they do it by coupling technical field specific skills with supplementary skills.

According to Burning Glass, in the modern US economy, the most valuable skill sets include two components. The first main component includes the technical (field specific) or core skills. For example, if your field is marketing, your core skills would be competitive analysis, market research, product marketing, and the like. The second component includes the non-field specific or supplementary skills. Data collected by Burning Glass overwhelmingly demonstrates that having supplementary skills, for example graphic design, search engine optimization, or business analytics, will almost double your employability and will likely get you a higher pay rate. Those findings were found to be consistent across multiple occupational fields including marketing, sales, computer programming, IT, general business, design, and social media.

In addition to the core and supplementary skills, the literature on employability recommends that you should also pay attention to generic or soft skills. Generic skills, which can also be called transferable skills, are those which are not specific to a particular job or industry but can be vital for the position in question. Generic skills typically include communication skills, teamwork, leadership, cross cultural competency, and project management. These days it is almost impossible to find a single job advertising without a requirement for a prospective employee to have for example, well-developed communication skills.

Now, we would like you to review the list of skills that you have identified for your current job. Suppose that you must select only five most important skills for the job including three core or field-specific skills, one supplementary or non-field specific skill, and one generic skill. We think that this exercise is useful for understanding skill sets and job requirements, and for focusing on the key competencies that are required for career growth in your area. After all, it is the key competencies that are getting evaluated by employers and recruiters in the process of competitive selection.

Competitive job selection plays a central role in our approach to measuring skills acquisition. A skill-based selection is a process where candidates' observable and perceived skills are evaluated, summarized, ranked, and compared. However imperfect this process may be, it seems to be the only working solution for measuring skills acquisition in real life.

The method that we are suggesting you use to imitate a competitive job selection in your area is called simulation. All we want you to do, is to participate in an imaginary job competition and imitate the work of a selection board, or a hiring manager, or even an HR recruiting robot powered by artificial intelligence. The simulation is intended to estimate your likely competitive ranking and a skill-based job selection process. The more realistic your simulation is, the more valid your results are supposed to be. Having some practical experience with competitive selection is crucial. This is why we recommend it as a prerequisite for this course. Ideally, with some experience, and maybe expert advice, you should be able to learn how to accurately predict your competitive scores.

To make it easier for you, we created a simple spreadsheet application, that you can use to run a simulation. In a moment, we'll introduce you to it, so you will be able to start practicing. Before you start practicing, let's quickly review what we have learned in this lecture.

First, to manage skills, we need to first measure them. Second, to measure job related skills, we should approach them as compact skill sets. Third, in the modern economy, skill sets are structured and include core, supplementary and complementary skills. Having the right skill set creates a competitive advantage. Fourth, in real life, skill sets are evaluated in the process of competitive selection. For training and development purposes, we can use a realistic simulation of a competitive selection.

Now, there is one last step to operationalize the concept of skills acquisition. We have established that we must delegate to the employer or recruiter, the task of an accurate and holistic evaluation of the skills of a prospective employee. But how do they typically do it?

You will need to find out in order to run a realistic simulation. To find an answer, you must consider the concept of skills acquisition from the employer's perspective. For an employer, it is not merely the skills of an applicant's resume that matter. What really matters, is how those skills are translated into the incumbent's performance on the job by accomplishing specific job-related tasks. Some tasks are more important than others, so employers would explicitly mention them in a job advertisement. Let's call them critical tasks. Critical tasks are often explicitly stated in the job advertising message. If not, employers would expect that you, a well-prepared applicant, have already learned about the expected critical tasks from your previous experience.

To unpack a job advertisement, you may need to do some research. This is another reason for you to become familiar with job market analytics such as those produced by Burning Glass. Here is the last exercise in this lecture. Can you translate the list of skills that you developed for your current job into the corresponding list of critical tasks? There may be more than one critical task per skill. As you can see on the screen, we selected an accounting job as an example. In the left column, we placed the skills that the prospective employee brings to the table. In the right column, we put corresponding critical tasks that the employer wants to be performed on the job. By translating skills into observable and measurable critical tasks, we complete the task of operationalizing skills. While it is difficult, if not impossible, to pinpoint and measure someone's mastery of skills in general, it is very practical to identify a list of critical tasks for each given job and use that as a proxy for the required skill set.

Works cited:

[1] Drucker, P. (2005). Managing Oneself. *Harvard Business Review*, January.
[2] www.burning-glass.com.

From external assessment to self-assessment

In Module 2, you were asked to specify a realistic job description, come up with a list of most appropriate selection criteria, and prepare a skills analysis by crafting a selection criteria statement and elaborating on your professional and generic capabilities, competencies and skills for the position. Now, it is time to review and discuss your application. Most importantly, how will a prospective employer read and evaluate it? To begin with, it seems to be a good idea to think about how the selection process usually works. You may want to get some additional information by browsing specialized websites and by googling <employee selection>.

From the employer's perspective, an employee selection process normally starts with the needs analysis and crafting a job advertising message where key competencies, skills, and experiences of a prospective employee are emphasized. As selection is typically a highly competitive process, key selection criteria are usually explicitly formulated to allow candidates prepare and submit an informative application package. Then, selection officers (or selection committee members) use scoring sheets to assign rankings to applicants' statements and credentials; if all selection criteria are met by a number of applicants, ranking helps choosing those candidates who seem to better fit for the job and can get through the initial screening for a face-to-face interview. After that, the selection process continues with presentations, interviews, demonstrations by invited candidates to select the best candidate for the job; those events are usually attended and assessed by designated officers (committee members). Overall, it's all about revealing and comparing pieces of the candidates' evidence of mastery in performing required skills.

As an example, you may find it useful to review the HRSG website: https://www.hrsg.ca/job-descriptions. HRSG is a Canadian HR company specializing in preparing job descriptions. For a candidate, a clear understanding of how selection process works can be very helpful in their job search and preparation. From a practical perspective, an ability "to put yourself in their shoes", i.e., seeing her/his application through the lens of selection committee, with a list of selection criteria and a ranking sheet in mind, is itself a valuable skill to complement job-seeking strategies. At the same time, an ability to develop an objective and critical ("outside") view of oneself adds up to self-awareness, self-analysis and self-management. By developing an external perspective, the candidate will learn how to see her/his unique combination of knowledge and skills in a competitive environment where all capabilities and their combination have to be pinpointed, demonstrated, proved, benchmarked, and rated. Also, the use of an outside, objective perspective validates self- assessment and ensures the integrity of the process. That's why in the reminder of this course we suggest that you "internalize" a prospective employer's external view of yourself and from that objective perspective critically review and thoroughly examine your own capabilities, knowledge and skills base, and performance.

Now, with this external perspective in mind, we suggest that you act as a prospective employer and engage in reviewing your own job application. As the employer, you are supposed to know very well about the most important skills that are required for the position (let's use the term Critical Skills Areas, or CSA). How would you approach the process of assessment? It seems logical to look for CSAs in the application; then, collect, observe and assess evidence of the candidate's preparation and performance using a ranking sheet. To do so, you will need a collection of assessment tools and some kind of methodology and experience in using the tools. As a result, you'll be able to gather and organize evidence, conduct a thorough investigation and come up with a meaningful, objective conclusion.

In Discussion D3 you are asked to reflect on your skills analysis in A2 by taking an employer's point of view. How would you rate your own application? What are your chances to get the job? Why? How can you make yourself the best candidate? How could you improve your job application? How can it inform your self-analysis?

Here is an additional source that you may find very useful to understand how personnel selection works:

- Highhouse, S., Doverspike, D., & Guion, R. (2016). *Essentials of Personnel Assessment and Selection*. 2nd ed. Routledge: New York.

How to approach self-assessment

Taking an external ("an employer's") perspective provides with a valid objective approach to self-analysis and self-assessment in a competitive environment. As in the previous part on self-analysis, we'll be drawing from different streams of literature. In the educational psychology and vocational training literature we can find well-developed approaches to gathering and organizing evidence and conducting self-assessment with the use of special tools (rubrics, checklists, observations, etc.). In the business strategy literature, we can find approaches to self-assessment designed for use in a competitive environment.

Self-assessment as a student's self-developmental strategy

The central role self-assessment plays in developing self-developmental strategies is emphasized by Georgina Loacker of Alverno College when she quoted one of her students saying that '*You have to be able to have an accurate idea of where you are and how you are doing...It's very difficult...unless you are able to figure out how it is that you are doing and that takes practice to get accurate and realistic*' (Loacker, 2003). In the same article, she defined self-assessment as "*not merely a matter of self-grading, nor an occasional summative analysis of a series of one's performances. It is an ongoing process of evaluating one's performance in a way that makes it sustained and sustaining essential part of lifelong learning*". According to G. Loacker (2003), the seven concepts of self-assessment include the following:

1. The understanding and practice of self-assessment as a developmental process where initially a beginning student expects someone else (typically, the teacher) to take the initiative in recognizing problems and pointing out concrete evidence to the student to make judgments on her behavior/performance. Understanding of self-assessment increases with practice; typically, it takes a few years of consistent practice in self-assessment for a student to internalize standards of self-assessment.
2. A second concept is the use of observable performance as the basis or evidence for judgment. It is particularly important for students to discern patterns of strengths and weaknesses that can assist them in their plans for improvement.
3. The third concept deals with careful observation. The challenge of precise observation lies especially in the ability to separate one's self from actual performance. For this reason it is important to assist a student to understand that each self-assessment is an evaluation, not of the person, but of a performance in a specific context or a series of performances in various contexts.
4. For an understanding of one's observations, the fourth concept, a reflection, plays an essential role. Getting at the how and why of one's actions seems to be an obvious step to avoid leaping to judgment.
5. A fifth concept incorporated into self-assessment as a developing process is that of the use of criteria that are gradually internalized. A given student might know that effective organization is a criterion for good writing, but it takes some time to understand exactly what that means in performance, how context and audience require it to vary, and how one integrates its myriad nuances and varieties and levels of expression.

6. The development of criteria is enhanced by instructor and peer feedback, which is the sixth defining concept identified here as essential to the kind of self-assessment needed for lifelong learning. Through such feedback, a student expands his or her operational understanding of what constitutes effective performance. Feedback from instructors and peers can highlight points the student missed, can discover gaps in the student's analysis, can provide other perspectives from which to view a performance, and can raise questions that might lead to further understanding.
7. The final concept is planning for improvement. Clearly the process of careful observation and reflective judgment, if recorded, can provide valuable information for ongoing improvement. Specifically, it can assist students to transform vague hopes into realistic goal setting. A goal might be set for the next single performance until it becomes a habit or it might span a semester or year. In any case, it encourages the student to reexamine and verify his or her intuitive decisions as well as intentionally informed ones.

The issues of reliability, validity, and utility of self-assessment are discussed by John Ross in his article published by Practical Assessment, Research and Evaluation in 2006.

Self-assessment in a vocational setting

Vocational education and training is concerned with skills acquisition and assessment and thus can provide with well-developed approaches to self-assessment including methodologies, frameworks and tools. A good example is presented by "Innovation and Business Skills Australia" which is one of several councils designated by the Australian government for assessing vocational skills (http://www.ibsa.org.au). According to that approach, skills can be formally assessed and recognized as qualifications where a so-called **unit of competency** is the smallest unit that can be assessed and recognized. Units of competency are comprised of **elements of competency;** elements describe the essential outcomes of a unit of competency. For each element of competency, there are **performance criteria** and an **evidence guide**.

The described vocational approach can be very useful for self-assessment, as it provides with a well-developed framework and describes assessment methods and instruments. For example, the competency unit TAEASS502A '*Design and develop assessment tools*' consists of four elements of competency (determine focus of the assessment tool; design assessment tool; develop assessment tool and review and trial assessment tool). Each element of competency has 3-5 performance criteria; for example, the element '*Determine focus of the assessment tool*' has the following performance criteria: a) identify target group of candidates, purposes of assessment tool, and contexts in which the tool will be used; b) access relevant benchmarks for assessment and interpret them to establish evidence required to demonstrate competence; c) identify, access and interpret organizational, legal and ethical requirements for relevant contextualization guidelines; d) identify other related documentation to inform assessment for self-development. For all elements of competency, required basic skills and knowledge are identified.

Self-assessment for professional development

For the sake of brevity, professional development trainers oftentimes come up with a list of key skills/competencies comprised of elements of competency and suggest a simplified tool for self-assessment. One example is presented by Exeter University in UK.

Lessons from business strategy: Competitive benchmarking

To get a meaningful result from the self-assessment exercise one has to take benchmarking very seriously. If benchmarking is done poorly or not adequately, the results of self-assessment wouldn't be sufficiently informative for developing an objective picture of the person's real standing in the competitive selection. Neither will they help preparing for a competitive employment, nor will they provide with directions for an efficient self-improvement. That's why we have recommended taking an objective, external view on own skills repertoire and performance. But how can one increase the validity of benchmarking? Are there any lessons that can be taken from corporate benchmarking in the business world? Are there any models that are used by companies and organizations for self-assessment and can be used by individuals?

This is a highly interesting topic that we would like you to discuss in Discussion D3. How can a job seeker benefit from using proven business strategy methods and tools (for example, VRINE - or VRIO analysis) for self-assessment, and why? To learn more about VRIO analysis, you may use some of the popular strategic management resources like Strategic Management Insight (www.strategicmanagementinsight.com).

Let's see how a business strategist that is charged with conducting self-assessment of a company may approach the task. Usually, an educated strategist begins with identifying factors that are deemed to be critically important for the chosen industry/sector (also known as KSF – *key success factors*). KSF are those factors that are absolutely necessary *for any company* to succeed given the industry characteristics. For example, in the commercial aircraft industry any competitor must possess large amounts of capital and research and development capabilities as prerequisites; any company lacking those capabilities is doomed to fail. An elaborated KSF analysis is used to create a list of categories (dimensions) for benchmarking the company's capabilities against competitors. Once the list of KSFs is ready, the strategist will turn to internal analysis to identify the company's resources and capabilities. If you google *<strategic resources and capabilities analysis>*, you'll find several useful approaches and tools used in the corporate world for that purpose (for example, value chain analysis, distinctive and key competencies analysis, etc.). As a result of those analyses, a list of resources and capabilities ("skills") of the company in the given industry will appear. After that the strategist will engage in a meticulous benchmarking of the company's resources and capabilities against the industry standards/ best practices pinpointed earlier as KSFs. A very popular tool for benchmarking that is recommended for use in the corporate world is known as VRINE (or VRIO) analysis. VRINE is actually a sort of rubric (or a checklist) used for comparison with the industry's "gold standard"; for each of the company's resources and capabilities the strategist is supposed to find out if this resource (or capability) is truly Valuable,

Rare, Inimitable, Non-Substitutable and Exploitable. Ideally only VRINE-tested resources and capabilities with the highest scores should be included into the company's SWOT analysis as its true internal strengths. As we see, by using models and tools such as KSF, VRINE, SWOT the strategist can produce an objective and informative self-assessment report demonstrating how the company given its resources and capabilities is prepared to match the competition.

Assessment/self-assessment methods and tools

What tools are available?

In the previously referenced document by IBSA the authors mention a range of **assessment methods**, including observation in the workplace, observation in simulated work environment, fault finding, role-playing, construction of role-play, games, game construction, verbal questioning, verbal presentation to assessor, verbal presentation to assessor and audience, formal oral examination, oral examination with panel, interview, debate, production of audio/ visual and other multimedia application, production of slide tape series, production of audio, group discussion, formal examination, short-answer test, take home examination, open book test or examination, multiple-choice answer test, essay, free choice essay, project (can also include a work-based project), documents, third party reports, training records, portfolio. While most of these methods require that an assessor (or a group of assessors and peer-reviewers) is involved, many methods can be used for self-assessment. **Tools** recommended for assessment and self-assessment include the following: description/videotaping an exemplar performance; instructions to candidates and assessors; scenarios and outlines of roles and key steps or issues to be covered; a list of set questions or a bank of questions; a checklist for assessment; instructions/guidelines for designing questions; a marking scheme; model case studies for analysis, etc.

A detailed discussion of assessment/self-assessment strategies and tools in an academic setting in relation to work-integrating learning can be found in an article by Theresa Winchester-Seeto, Jacqueline Mackaway, Debra Coulson and Marina Harvey.

For practical purposes, most assessment/self-assessment procedures use criterion-referenced measures by matching the student's performance against a set of criteria and using a scoring scale (also known as **rubric**). A rubric typically consists of two components: criteria and levels of performance. As an example, you may want to take a look at the VALUE Rubric developed by the Association of American Colleges and Universities. Some of their rubrics can be used for self-assessment, particularly, rubrics for Written and Oral Communication, Teamwork, Life-long Learning. The rubric for assessing teamwork begins with a clear identification of what teamwork means and consists of five criteria (contribution to team meetings; facilitation of contribution to team meetings; individual contribution outside of team meetings; fostering constructive team climate and response to conflicts) and four performance levels with related descriptions of each level. Ideally, by using the rubric individuals are supposed not only to learn about expectations for skill acquisition and their current standing, but also receive a clear direction for improvement.

The advantage of using a well-developed rubric, with extensive and explicit descriptors for levels of performance, is that expectations for skill acquisition are clearly formulated, consistent, and objective; the disadvantage is that an accurate assessment takes time and should be done consistently. That's why a simplified approach is sometimes used where instead of descriptors only levels of performance are indicated (poor, good, excellent) or a nominal (yes-no) scale is used (**a checklist**). To understand how to construct and use a rubric, we recommend that you get familiar with Jon Mueller's Authentic Assessment Toolbox.

How to use assessment tools to self-evaluate graduate employability skills

Universities promoting graduate employability skills in their graduates use e-portfolios to gather and organize evidence of skills acquisition and assessment/self-assessment rubrics for evaluation/feedback purposes. A good example is presented by Deakin University in Australia where standard templates are provided to instructors and students to pinpoint and evidence achievement in critical skills areas such as communication skills, information technology skills, critical and analytical thinking, problem solving, working independently, teamwork, cross-cultural skills and diversity. The rubrics developed at Deakin can be used for self-assessment purposes.

A comprehensive long term project charged with making the match between university graduates and corporate employers is described in an article by Iris Berdrow and Frederick Evers (2011). The researchers defined a set of 17 skills combined in 4 distinct areas (managing self, communicating, managing people, mobilizing innovation and change) that captured the current base competencies necessary to succeed in a business career and then described a competency-based course (similar to this one) where students were required to develop their skills portfolio, perform self-assessment, work on a presentation of their skills and prepare a plan for improvement. Their self-assessment plan included 17 skills (learning, personal organization/time management, personal strengths, problem solving/analytic skills, interpersonal skills, listening, oral communication, written communication, coordinating, decision making, leadership/influence, managing conflict, planning and organizing, ability to conceptualize, creativity/innovation/change, risk taking, visioning), a description of elements of each competency, a simplified rubric for self-assessment, and provided room for self-reflection and goal setting for self-improvement.

How the approach taken in this course is different

In this course, we take a similar approach to the one described in the previous section; the difference is that in the above mentioned examples colleges deal with traditional age students' preparation and transition to work. Traditional age college students typically know significantly less about "real-world", competitive employment than adult students. That's why they are usually offered a broad spectrum of potentially useful employability skills derived for their consideration by researchers and professors; then, the students are asked to self-assess themselves based on their perceptions of mastery/preparedness in the suggested skills areas. As a proxy for future competitive selection experiences, this seems to be a valid approach, but still it is an academic exercise and is not the same as a real life experience. In this course we primarily target adult students, i.e. those with significantly more experience in gaining competitive employment. That's why we have suggested students to specify a description for the position that they are familiar with and are interested in and then to identify a list of selection criteria and related competencies/skills including critical skills areas for the particular job. The resultant lists of CSAs are individualized and supposed to include only those items that truly matters for the students to get the job in a real life setting. The advantage of this approach is that it is more practical and job-related; also, it requires students to concentrate on fewer, more important skills in their particular situation. The disadvantage is that we cannot use a cookie cutter approach and use ready-made lists of skills, with detailed definitions, descriptors and rubrics. Ideally, based on the materials presented in this content guide and suggested readings, you should be able to come up with a list and definitions of CSAs relevant to your particular situation, identify related competency elements, develop descriptors, collect evidence of their performance, identify benchmarks/best practices, design rubrics and conduct self-assessment. Once the students will have mastered this approach, they will be able to use it continuously for finding employment, getting promotion and self-improving.

The E-Portfolio task CPW3 in this Module is designed to help mastering self-assessment for use in a competitive job market environment. Assignment A3 is a useful exercise that is designed to help organizing and explaining students' work and to provide avenue for constructive feedback.

References:

- *Australian Government, Department of Education, Employment and Workplace Relations* (2012). TAEASS502A Design and develop assessment tools.
- Berdrow I., Evers F.T. (2011). Bases of competence: A framework for facilitating reflective learner-centered educational environments. *Journal of Management Education*, 35 (3), 406-427.
- Loacker, J. (2003). Taking Self-Assessment Seriously. *Essays on Teaching Excellence toward the Best in the Academy, 15(2)*. The Vanderbilt Center for Teaching.
- Mueller, J. (2010). *Authentic Assessment Toolbox*. Available online at http://jfmueller.faculty.noctrl.edu/toolbox/
- *National Quality Council (2009).* Guide for Developing Assessment Tools. Victoria, Australia.
- Ross, J. A. (2006). The Reliability, Validity, and Utility of Self-Assessment. *Practical Assessment Research & Evaluation*, 11(10).
- Winchester-Seeto, T., Mackaway, J., Coulson, D. & Harvey, M. (2010). 'But how do we assess it?' An analysis of assessment strategies for learning through participation (LTP). *Asia-Pacific Journal of Cooperative Education*, 11(3), 67-91.

Discussion D3: Are you the best candidate for the job/promotion?

Now, it is time to review your Selection Criteria Statement that you just submitted in Module 2 (Assignment A2-2). Here is the scenario: Suppose you are the employer and there are several, possibly too many applicants for the job that you have advertised through a job search website. Suppose that you cannot meet with the applicants in person and all you've got is a bunch of applications with their resumes and responses to the selection criteria.

In your main post in this discussion, we would like you to answer the following questions:

1. *If you were the employer, how would you rate your own application? Would you employ yourself? Why?*
2. *How can you become the best candidate for the job? How could you strengthen your job application?*
3. *Why taking an external (the employer's or a peer reviewer's) perspective on one's skills is helpful when seeking jobs? Why an ability to objectively assess skills is important for self-improvement?*
4. *How can a job seeker benefit from using business strategy methods and tools (for example, VRINE - or VRIO - analysis) for self-assessment, and why?*

To learn more about VRIO analysis, you may use some of the popular strategic management resources like Strategic Management Insight. Also, review the relevant chapters in the textbook and optional Coursera videos.

Further readings on business strategy:

- Hoskisson, R.E., Hitt, M.A., Ireland, R.D., & Harrison, J.S. (2013). *Competing for Advantage*. 3rd ed. Mason, OH: South-Western, Cengage Learning.
- Porter, M.E. (1980). *Competitive Strategy.* New York, The Free Press.
- Porter, M.E. (1985). *Competitive Advantage.* New York, The Free Press.
- Prahalad, C.; Hamel, G. (1990). The core competence of the corporation. *Harvard Business Review, 68, 79–91.*
- Wheelen, T., Hunger, J. Hoffman, A., & Bamford, C. (2015). *Strategic Management and Business Policy: Globalization, Innovation, and Sustainability.* 14th ed. Pearson.

Module M4:

Managing Your Skills Lab

Overview

The goal of Module 4 is to organize your findings and make sense of self-assessment. You will learn how to objectively evaluate your T.S.S. (the Total Skillset Score) for a given position.

In this Module, you will continue examining the use of performance management tools and techniques for individual skills management. By the end of the Module, you will quantify your level of skills acquisition and objectively estimate your likely T.S.S. (The Total Skillset Score) for the given job in a competitive job selection process (the one you specified in Module 2). In the beginning of the Module, you will examine theoretical and practical approaches to identifying and analyzing job-related skillsets. Then, you will continue exploring the use of performance management techniques for skills assessment. As a result, you will be able to quantify your level of skills acquisition for the chosen position and come up with a realistic estimate for your likely T.S.S. supported by the Critical Skills Dashboard. In addition, you will create a process for: 1) collecting evidence of your mastery in performing job-specific skills; 2) soliciting and documenting expert and peer-assessment of the level of your skills acquisition. In the end of the Module, we will ask you to review your Critical Skills Dashboard and compare it with the results of your prior SWOT analysis. As self-assessment is the most convenient but the least objective method of skills assessment, we will ask you to think about how to make your self-assessment more accurate, valid, and reliable.

Module Learning Objectives:

M4-1	Review theoretical and practical approaches to identifying and analyzing job-related skillsets.	**R4**
M4-2	Continue working on the implementation of performance management methods and techniques for the quantification of your level of skills acquisition as related to the identified skillset for the chosen position.	**CPW4**
M4-3	Engage in the process of skills assessment by soliciting peer- and expert evaluation and conducting self-assessment of the skills in your skillset for the chosen position.	**D4, CPW4**
M4-4	Develop a process for collecting evidence of your mastery in performing job-specific skills and soliciting and documenting expert and peer-assessment of the level of your skills acquisition.	**CPW4**
M4-5	Synthesize and review your findings in the Module using the provided Critical Skills Dashboard, calculate and analyze your T.S.S.	**A4-1**
M4-6	Review theoretical foundations of self-assessment and reflect on your experience in self-assessing your skills.	**A4-2**

Let's review where we are in the course

This course is intended to provide students with the necessary methodology and tools for career growth and puts emphasis on career self-management as the key meta-skill. In Modules 2-3 you have learned how to approach and conduct the foundational steps in self-management, namely self-analysis and self-assessment, in a competitive job market context. In particular, you have examined relevant psychological theories and concepts. Also, methods and tools used by business strategists, and approaches to self-assessment suggested in vocational training literature. To combine theory and practice, you have identified your own professional and generic competencies and skills that seem to be most valued by employers in your chosen field; then, you have engaged in collecting relevant evidence of your actual mastery of performing job-related skills and measuring it against benchmarks. To do so, you have started using self-management tools like self-observation and self-reflection instruments (learning journal), self-assessment instruments (rubrics, checklists), monitoring tools (dashboard and e-portfolio). In Module 4, you are supposed to review and organize your findings to make sure that you can use career self-management knowledge and skills to guide your ongoing professional development and personal growth in future.

Your personal lab

By now, we have introduced enough instruments to create a well-equipped self-developmental lab. Does one really need to have a learning journal, an e-portfolio, a collection of evidence of your own performance and best practices, a range of tools for self-assessment, a collection of skill-builders, a monitoring device (dashboard)? Does it sound like another full-time job? Do we have enough trouble without it?

A simple answer is that there are some tools that are continuously used in professional life anyway; for example, resumes, CVs, short bios, presentations, professional portfolios, LinkedIn accounts, references, diaries, self-help books, etc. The approach taken in this course builds on those practices and suggests a way to integrate various tools and take advantage of efforts of many theorists and practitioners concerned with the development of employability skills.

In a nutshell, your personal self-development lab is a place (real or imaginary) where you can pinpoint your skills and measure them against the competition to answer the following questions: What do I really know and what can I do? What can I do better than potential candidates and where should I improve? What are my real strengths and weaknesses? What are threats and opportunities? What are my options? How should I improve my skills? Which courses should I take and why? What level should I be able to achieve, why and how?

Critical Skills Dashboard: an instrument for career self-management

In this course, we build on existing theories and reported approaches and suggest using certain self-assessments tools and a dashboard as a self-reporting and self-monitoring tool. It can certainly be further adjusted to individual needs. For example, some HR development consultants suggest using a personal balanced scoring card. The dashboard can easily be incorporated into this approach.

Making sense of skills assessment

In this section, you will finalize the work on Critical Skills Dashboard in your E-Portfolio and Learning Journal Workbook (CPW4).

Your competitive standing

The main idea behind the Dashboard is to provide you with a clear and honest picture of your likely competitive standing in relation to potential candidates for the position specified in Module 2 Assignment 2.

If this is a job of your dream that you think you may be able to get at some point, your dashboard is supposed to tell you where you are and what needs to be done in order to improve your position in the future and get that or a similar job. What is particularly important is that your dashboard is not a product of wishful thinking, but on the contrary it is based on a solid evidentiary base of your own performance and best practices/standards in the field.

Identifying gaps and parities

The Dashboard is designed to provide a clear picture of your strengths and weaknesses; as such, it can be very instrumental in the development of personal strategies aimed at building on strengths and eliminating weaknesses. For example, it demonstrates which particular skills and competencies can be considered "demonstrated strengths" and should be emphasized in your self-marketing strategy and in a job application/interview (more in the next Module). Also, it tells about particular skills that needs improvement (more on self-development in Module 6).

How accurate is the Dashboard?

Like any tool, the Dashboard's accuracy completely depends on the quality of the information collected and self-assessment results obtained. There are two rather difficult tasks involved in constructing a personal dashboard including: a) identification of the relevant standards/best practices and obtaining examples and b) conducting the self-assessment. The question is whether students can do it on their own, without some (or significant help) from experienced academics, mentors, consultants, or trainers. The whole idea of lifelong, self-directed learning is that in the 21st century the only way to succeed is to become self-independent, self-taught and self-managed. To do so, one needs to develop necessary competencies in self-regulated learning (see more in Modules 2 and 3). One of the characteristics of self-regulated learners is that they actively seek and know how to use constructive feedback from professionals and peers.

The Total Skillset Score

When considering applicants for a job, employers often norm selection criteria by assigning numerical weights. Let us see how it is done in the provided CSD. Please note that the total of weights is 100 meaning that an ideal candidate for the job will score 100 points. Now, we can calculate the T.S.S. (or the Total Skillset Score) for any candidate if we know their subscores (performance levels). If, for example, the weight of Written Communications is 20% and the candidate's performance level is 2 (out of 4), then the subscore for Written Communications is 10 (out of 20). In the example provided the T.T.S. of the prospective candidate is 66.5 which clearly indicates that there is plenty of room for growth. If you were the candidate, how would you calculate your T.S.S.?

VIDEO LECTURE: What is Your Total Skillset Score?

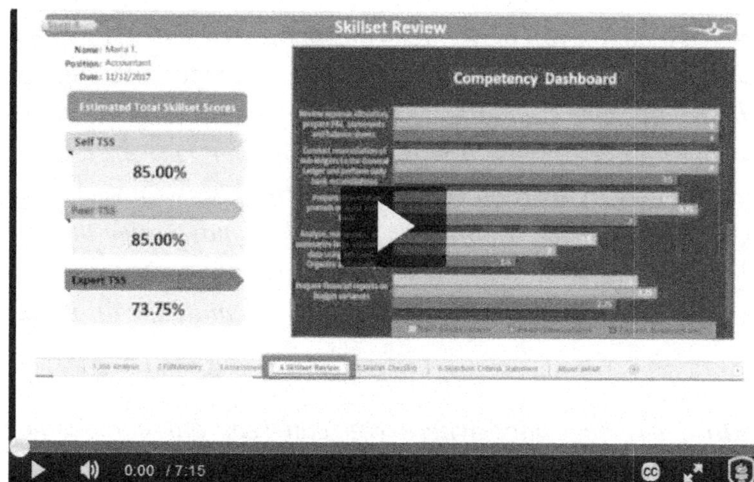

This video lecture is taken from "How to Get Skilled", an advanced level Coursera course for working professionals filmed in 2018. In the lecture, we describe the computation and discuss practical uses of the Total Skillset Score (T.S.S.). Also, we are using a special application (called "JAFAR"). We think that this presentation is a useful illustration of the concepts in this course. Though, in the course we do not use the application. Instead, you are using CSAT which basically does the same. In Module 7 we will explain how you can get access to the application for your ongoing self-developmental work.

© The text and slides in this video are prepared by Professor Val Chukhlomin, narration by Amy Giaculli, videography by John Hughes, animation by Alena Rodick, and editing by Dr. Dana Gliserman-Kopans (2018).

In this lecture, we will continue the conversation about science and art of measuring skills. You are already familiar with the app we developed for this course. Now it's time to give it a test drive so you can see how it can help you manage, develop, and present your skills to current and prospective employers.

In the previous lecture, we detailed how you can organize your skills by clustering them around specific jobs. To illustrate our point, we used an example with an accounting job. We also asked you to think about how to create a job specific skillset for your current job. If you did it, you can now find the resultant skill set on the job analysis page tab one in the app. Now, let's click through the entire app. There are only six pages, so you can see what it's all about.

To begin, click on tab two. Tab two brings you to the full mastery page. This is where all standard requirements, expectations, and best practices for the job are stored. The ideal applicant is supposed to know and be proficient at all of these to be competitive in the job application process. Next is tab three, assessment. This page includes descriptions of or links to available evidence of your mastery in the field and also methods of assessment. As you can see, for a specific job, instead of measuring skills in general, it makes sense to assess your level of mastery in performing each of the critical tasks. The assessment should ideally be done by an expert evaluator, but you can also use peer assessment or self-assessment as a proxy.

Do you want to see how it works? To begin, you may enter your perceived self-assessment scores for each of the critical tasks that you have identified for your current job. We suggest that you use a scale of zero to four and score yourself according to the rubric on the right-hand side. For example, you should enter a three if you think that your current level is advanced, and you perform the task exactly as required in most situations with very little supervision or oversight. What else is important about this page? You may notice that we normed all skills equally in the column called weights. If you wish, you can adjust it as you see fit for your current job. Norming is useful as it will allow you to calculate the total skill set score on the next page.

Tab four brings you to the skill set review page where you can see your competency dashboard and the estimated total skillset score. In our case, it is solely based on self-assessment. If you correctly identified the required skill set, and accurately self-assessed your levels of proficiency, this page is supposed to tell you what your current standing is in relation to the job requirements. Also, the competency dashboard informs you about your strengths and competency gaps. To make your total skill set score more accurate, you should be looking for ways to get your mastery of performing critical tasks assessed by peers and ideally, by an expert evaluator. This way, you'll get valid numbers. We'll talk more about it in the next lecture. Now, let's keep moving to see what is on the next page.

Page five gives you the summary of your skillset checklist. This is a big picture of your combined level of skills acquisition for the job. Once it is fully completed, you can print it and use it for a conversation with your supervisor or a career coach. You can also be your own self coach and help yourself with identifying training needs and smart goals.

Before we proceed to tab six, there is one question I wanted to ask you. Do you feel that what we are showing to you looks somewhat familiar? This may well be the case if you work in a corporate environment and your organization is using some form of performance management. In this case, your organization is likely to constantly monitor your competencies and skills. So, you may already know what your current level of mastery is and what your supervisor wants you to accomplish in terms of professional development. These days, there are many HR technologies that help organizations to manage skills of their employees. As mentioned earlier, what we are doing in this course is indeed inspired by HR practices in the business world.

But there is also a very significant difference in the way we approach professional development. Just think about it. When a company manages your skills, it considers you part of their human capital. That's why the HR systems are designed to only develop the skills that are necessary for the business. This can be very useful for you, but it may also prove to be insufficient in the long term, don't you think? For example, you will probably lose access to the system after you leave the job. Also, it is not likely that you would be able to use the company's performance management system to hone the skills for career change. And how about preparing job applications for a different employer?

What we are trying to say is that you may need a backup plan for nurturing skills for your continuing employability. We want to empower you as an individual, a skilled professional, and the master of skills. Don't you want to be in full control of your skills, so you do not lose any opportunities in the wider world? This was well said wasn't it? Okay, it's time to prove it.

At this point, in addition to all performance management and career development knowledge, I will probably need some old school magic. To do so, I will rub this old lamp and you should click on tab six. You see, all information that has been entered and processed in the app is now showing in the template for writing a powerful selection criteria statement for your next career move. This way, all your skill building self-development work contributes to an evidence based and data driven document that is meant to better prepare you for your next job application and interview. We'll talk more about it in the tangible outcomes lecture. But before proceeding to tangible outcomes, we shall discuss how to populate the app with accurate and valid data. As a proven magician, David Copperfield once said, "The real secret of magic lies in the preparation."

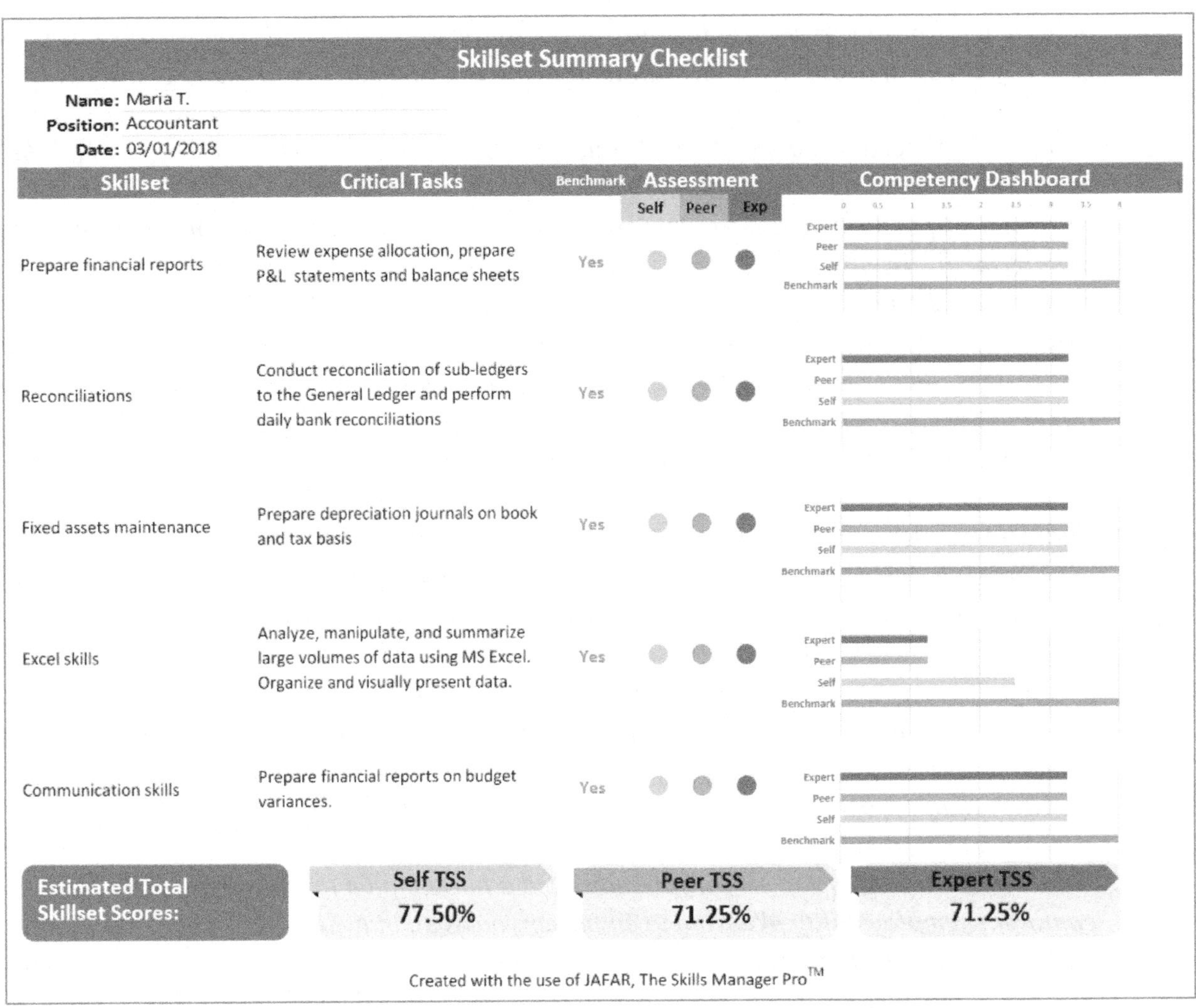

Figure 2: Skillset Summary Checklist

Figure 2 provides an illustration of the skillset summary checklist created with the use of JAFAR. *JAFAR, The Skills Manager Pro ®* is an application that is used for calculating T.S.S. in "How to Get Skilled" on Coursera. The application uses the same logic as the CSAT tool in this course and helps organize and presents the results of skills assessment. As you can see in this illustration, the chosen position of accountant includes five key competencies ("Prepare financial reports", "Reconciliations", "Fixed Assets Maintenance", Excel skills", and "Communication Skills"). For each of the key competencies, there are corresponding Critical Tasks. For each of the critical tasks, the student identified a corresponding benchmark and obtained three types of skill assessment (self-, peer- and expert). Competency dashboards are presented for each skill, as well T.S.S. are calculated for each type of skill assessment. In this course, you learn how to do the same work in a step-by-step manner, using CSAT and CSD. In the future, you can easily switch to using JAFAR to automate some of your calculations. Also, JAFAR can help you translate your self-developmental work into tangible outcomes (see Figure 3 on the next page).

Selection Criteria Statement

Name: Maria T.
Position: Accountant
Date: 03/01/2018

Skill	Critical Task(s)
Prepare financial reports	**Review expense allocation, prepare P&L statements and balance sheets**

Evidence:

- Job references & Internal papers
- Published annual audited reports

Evidence Notes:

- 5 years experience producing Board of Director's papers at Smith and Co***;
- Preparation of reports for Gregory Dunn, Inc*** as noted in the published annual report by the CFO;
- Reduction of variances due to revision of payables procedures to ensure correct cost allocation at Bars, LLC.***

Assessment Results: (0-4 Rating Scale)	Self-Assessment	Peer-Assessment	Expert Assessment
	3.25	**3.25**	**3.25**

Assessment Notes:

Peer assessment - by colleagues at Smith and Co***;
Expert assessment - by the CFO at Bars LLC.***

Benchmark:

Compliance with accounting standards and internal policies and procedures.

Benchmarking Criteria:

Data is systematically checked for accuracy and reliability. Balance Sheet, Profit and Loss statements are prepared in accordance with statutory and organizational requirements. Errors identified and corrected, or referred for resolution in accordance with orgnaizational policy and procedures. Information is prepared for internal and external auditors.

Created with the use of JAFAR, The Skills Manager Pro™

Figure 3: Selection Criteria Statement

Discussion D4: Can you outsmart a recruiting robot?

In modern days, job selection is increasingly getting automated by AI (Artificial Intelligence) where AI-powered robots scan the profiles of prospective applicants and rank them based on assigned numerical scores.

What would be your strategy for getting the highest possible score when dealing with an AI-powered job search engine? Can you realistically "guestimate" your likely score in any job selection process? Can you think of a smart strategy that can get you a higher score?

Before responding, review the following video. Please make sure that in your responses you reflect on your work in the Workbook.

Module M5:

Transformation: Self-Marketing and Personal Branding

Overview

The goal of the Module is to learn how you can effectively present your mastery of skills and market yourself professionally.

In the Module, you will engage in creating, organizing, and exhibiting artifacts demonstrating evidence of your mastery of skills for successful job search/promotion. You will examine methods and techniques originally developed by specialists in professional services marketing and promotion of human brands. As self-marketing is a complex career competency in itself, you will begin the Module by examining the underpinning knowledge, skills, and attitudes. Then, you will focus on developing mastery in documenting your skills and communicating them to various audiences using networking and impression management. Drawing on models, methods, and techniques derived from strategic marketing, you will establish a process for identifying and documenting your skills and practice in showcasing and communicating them in the form of an elevator pitch on You Tube.

Module Learning Objectives:

M5-1	Review theoretical foundations of professional services marketing and human branding and discuss their applicability for establishing and promoting your Professional Brand (The Skilled Self).	**R5, D5**
M5-2	Analyze self-marketing and personal branding as a key career competency (The 7P Framework) in the context of a competitive job selection and formulate a sound self-promotional strategy.	**CPW5**
M5-3	Analyze your self-marketing capability as a job-related skill by identifying and self-assessing underlying competency units/elements and critical tasks.	**CPW5**
M5-4	Develop Self-Marketing and Personal Branding Plan.	**A5-1**
M5-5	Apply the relevant elements of marketing communications mix for creating an elevator pitch on You Tube.	**A5-2**
M5-6	Synthesize elements of your self-promotional strategy and incorporate them into a functional resume and a LinkedIn professional profile (optional).	**CPW5**

VIDEO LECTURE: Introduction to Career Branding

This video provides an introduction to the theme of Self-Marketing and Personal Branding. It was filmed for "*Career Brand Management*" specialization on Coursera in 2016.

© The text and slides are prepared by Val Chukhlomin, narration by Amy Giaculli (2016). Image credits: Shuttterstock.com

Please note that in this video we refer to courses on Coursera that follow the same logic as this course, though the sequence of activities is slightly different.

Hi, I'm Amy Giaculli. In this final course of the Career Brand Management specialization, we'll explore strategic self-marketing and personal branding. The goal of this course is to help you showcase your skills to prospective employers and other interested parties such as your colleagues, supervisors, or if you're an entrepreneur, potential investors and customers. To accomplish this goal, we'll need to closely examine the concepts of career brand and branding.

As you may recall from the previous course, a person's career brand is not how the person sees himself or herself. A career brand is a perception of the person's skills and capabilities in the minds of other people, most notably, employers and colleagues. We can also call it a professional reputation, or professional image. Traditionally, personal branding was reserved for celebrities such as royalties, politicians, athletes, and artists. But with the arrival of the Internet and social media, almost everyone has obtained a digital identity and can now use branding tools and techniques for self-promotion. In this course we'll focus on career branding.

To begin, let's think about how career branding actually works. Like any other brand, a career brand is meant to create in the customer's mind a point of differentiation with other brands or unbranded products. A career brand works as an inner voice telling the employer, choose that person, and this is the one I really want to get on board. Career developers can actively form their brands by creating and promoting their digital identities to prospective employers. But the problem is that all job candidates may be sending the same kind of signals to employers.

To understand how the receiver's mind processes those signals, let's think about how employers actually make hiring decisions. Interestingly, the way employers handle selection seems not to be very different from what consumers do when buying a complex product or service. Initially, they both scan either applications or available offerings, looking for desired characteristics or skills. As a result, they select a group of comparable offerings or job applicants that best fit the requirements. The model of skill-based selection that we examined in course one describes this process very well.

The same model also allowed us to demonstrate how using skill building tools and techniques can help candidates excel in competitive selection and get into the selection playoffs so to speak. What happens next when employers or consumers face a problem of making a choice between the few remaining candidates or products with comparable characteristics? The candidates that made it to the selection playoffs are probably very good, or excellent, or even exceptional in terms of acquired functional skills. To win the race, a successful candidate will need to make the most distinct impression, so the selection team will feel that by selecting the particular person, they're making the right choice.

This is where we need to switch from the functional to the emotional side of career branding. On the emotional side, career branding is all about building a powerful professional image for promoting one's self in the crowded marketplace. It can be achieved by building a professional reputation and purposefully crafting the desired image and then communicating it through impression management. By doing so, job applicants attract attention, create interest, develop trust, establish relationships, and ignite a positive emotion. Through reputation management and impression management, a successful job applicant helps to create a positive image of his or her skills and capabilities in the employer's mind by connecting the unknown with what they already know and see favorably. The intended result is a positive hiring attitude leading to a good job offer. Because this is similar to what companies do when they promote their products or services to prospective buyers and want them to become loyal and devoted followers.

Let's look closely at how companies actually do it and figure out what we can learn from that and use for career branding. In the business world, companies use marketing strategies and techniques to push their products and services to consumers through promotion, advertising, and by other available means. They also pull their products and services by helping consumers create desired brand images and link them to personal values, aspirations, and attributes. Brands help instantly transmit complex messages and transform them into positive emotions in the consumer's mind. As a result, for a happy customer a branded product or service becomes more than just the sum of the physical attributes. It brings value, trust, harmony, and peace of mind.

There's a lot of research on marketing and branding in the commercial world, and it is certainly of interest to draw on that literature, to see what may be useful for individual career development. The intended result of career branding efforts is a strong career brand. Eventually, it should lead to career growth. A strong brand is one that is based on a strong skills portfolio and reinforced by a powerful personal image. Both components should be in place. Otherwise, if skills are strong but not promoted as needed the resultant brand is generic and may undermine career growth. On the other hand, if a personal image is being heavily promoted but not rooted in real skills, that brand is going to be inflated, unstable and may quickly vanish.

In this course, we'll focus on building a powerful personal image and answer the following questions. What can we learn from business strategy about marketing and brands? How can we develop a sound self-marketing strategy? How does personal branding work? How can we use impression management? There are four weeks in this course. In week one we'll examine career brand management as a skill that any career developer should master. In week two we'll focus on self-marketing strategies and tactics. Basically, this is about what you can take from business strategy and implement in a career self-development context. Week three is dedicated to personal branding. This is where we'll try to get into the employer's mind and see how you can proactively manage your image. Finally, we'll review the entire specialization in week four.

During the course, we'll continue working in the career development lab. And we'll be relying on the self-coaching tools introduced in previous courses, such as the skill building dashboard, t portfolio, the self-assessment grid. We'll also introduce new tools, such as the Showcaser and the brand equity builder. But before we do it, we'll need you to think about your desired professional image and the brand promise that you're going to deliver to the prospective employer. Previously, we talked about your future work self in terms of desired competencies and skills. Now it is time to think about how to package and showcase your skills and make sure that the employers, colleagues, supervisors, investors and all other interested parties get the message and act on it. Are you ready? Let's get started.

Self-Marketing as a Career Competency: The 7P Framework

You can significantly improve your self-marketing skills, if you begin thinking about them as an important career competency. To approach self-marketing more professionally, you can learn a lot from the discipline of marketing. Of particular interest is the field known as "professional services marketing". The foundational model of services marketing is called 7P, as it describes the seven, most important components of services marketing (product, price, place, promotion, people, processes, and physical evidence). Now, if you used the same 7P framework for self-marketing of your skills when applying for the position you specified in Module 2, what would be the most important factors for you to consider? To answer this question, we recommend that you populate the table below. Once again, please note that this is not a one-size-fits-all approach. In other words, for each position the 7P table needs to be slightly (or significantly) modified.

	7 P components	**Description**	**How to use: strategies and tools**
1	Product/service	<You are your skills. Define here your skillset for the job>	Current credentials, experiences, functional resume, bio sketch
2	Price/value	You are selling not yourself but your skills as a solution to the employer's problems.	Your USP – think about how to incorporate it in your cover letter and during your job interview
3	Place/Positioning	Your skills need to closely match the job requirements.	Selection criteria statement, covering letter, certifications

4	Promotional mix and packaging	This is how you showcase and demonstrate your skills.	LinkedIn, recorded presentations, professional publications.
5	People	There must be other people to support your claims.	Networking, social media, job references, peer reviews
6	Physical evidence	Hard evidence + argument = the best proof of your skills	Selection criteria statement, work samples, other evidence
7	Process/Productivity	You need to be a team player, with a growth mindset.	Think how to show personal skills and a positive attitude.

Creating a powerful personal brand

Now, your competitive strengths as reported in the Dashboard and supported by evidence in the e-portfolio need to be converted into unique selling points (USP). To do so, it is useful to find out about how generic strategies are usually implemented in the business world. Particularly, how generic strategies are supplemented by functional strategies, including marketing strategies. You may want to begin by googling <marketing strategy>. It is likely that you'll find out resources and articles on branding and brand management, including personal branding. We suggest that you discuss related issues in Discussion 5.

VIDEO LECTURE: The Skilled Self as a Product

This video explains how you can approach marketing your skilled self professionally. The video was prepared for "Career Brand Management" specialization on Coursera.

© The text and slides are prepared by Val Chukhlomin, narration by Amy Giaculli. Image credits: Shuttterstock.com (2016)

Please note that in this video we refer to courses on Coursera that follow the same logic as this course, though the sequence of activities is slightly different.

Hello again. In this presentation, we'll discuss the product that you're going to bring to the market, the Self. Interestingly, there are many possible selves, depending on the social context each person may assume different identities. For example, the same person can have one identity for dating on the web. And use another for work related activities. Even professional identities can be different. For example, one identity as an employer, and another as an entrepreneur. So how shall we define the self in this course?

In previous courses, we mainly focused on individual, work-related characteristics and examined the concept of future work self. A person's future work self, is his or herself image of desired work-related characteristics. A future work self, is his or her vision for the knowledge, skills, and abilities to acquire for career growth. As we discussed earlier, if you are interested in purposefully building your skills and capabilities a clear vision of your future work self may serve as a blueprint for your own self development.

When you are thinking about career growth, you must take into account how your skills and capabilities are perceived by other people. If you are a skilled person, then the more employers know and appreciate your mastery in a certain field, the likelier they will be to hire you and the better your career prospects should be. Wouldn't it be great if you could control or at least influence the way other people see you? Or we may put it this way. Can one manage his or her own professional image by regulating impressions that other people develop about his or her work-related skills and capabilities?

In this course we'll explore how you, a career developer, can design a desired professional image and use marketing and branding tools and techniques to communicate it to prospective employers and other interested parties. As skills and capabilities are the central elements of your desired professional image. Let's call the product that you are bringing to the market the skilled self.

For this product, prospective employers, colleagues, supervisors can all be considered customers. What you want to do is correctly position yourself in the minds of your target audience. And use a variety of push and pull strategies to deliver your message, and eventually get hired and reach your career goals. Push strategies will include self-marketing techniques such as advertising, promotion, direct selling, and public relations. Pull strategies will include personal branding and impression management.

As your customers are simultaneously exposed to promotional messages that are sent by many other job seekers and career developers, your goal is to stand out and make sure that your vision of yourself as the skilled self adequately translates into their impression of you as the preferred candidate. So, the skilled self is a desired professional image of one's self that a job applicant or a career developer designs and then needs to transmit to the target audience and make sure that it is adequately translated by them.

Can you think about the desired professional image that you want to transmit to your target audience? How would you describe it? You may find that designing and transmitting a desired professional image Is not a very easy undertaking as people may say things differently than you do. Also, the message to be transmitted can be quite complex and will most likely include several layers of information. Let's see what those layers are.

The fundamental layer includes information about one's personality traits and personal attributes and is deeply rooted in the person's values, beliefs learning and thinking styles and cultural identification. This is the very core of who the person is. You may call this layer the Core Self. One's core qualities underpin and augment skills development. For example, an ability to be a quick learner, or work under pressure or be creative. In course one, we discussed personality traits in more detail. In this course, we should think about how to package them, and present, as part of your desired professional image.

In the process of education training, and professional growth, an individual develops his, or her, inner self by adding to it a layer of competencies consisting of new knowledge, skills and abilities. As a result, here she becomes a carrier of marketable skills, at least in the eyes of prospective employers. This is what we called the skilled self. And what a career developer brings to the job market. But how would employers and other interested parties know about what is hidden inside of you?

Degrees and diplomas can provide information about education, but how can one package and present his or her skills and abilities? To make one's skills and abilities visible to outside parties, the person needs to create a layer of artifacts. An artifact is a physical object such as a document, image, certificate, plaque or a sign or a digital object such as website, e-portfolio or a badge. Artifacts serve as evidence of one's mastery in a chosen field. You can think of artifacts as extensions of your skilled self that are visible, verifiable and clearly understood by your target audiences.

In many professional occupations, the need for creating extended skilled selves, was recognized a long time ago. For example, when visiting a doctor's office, you can find an office plaque with the doctor's credentials on the wall. What do you think is the purpose of that artifact? What is it supposed to tell you? What is your impression when you've visited a doctor's office for the first time?

In today's digitized world, almost everyone has obtained a digital identity, which is based on digital artifacts. Digital artifacts include electronic resumes, LinkedIn and Facebook profiles, e-portfolios, websites, blogs, Twitter SlideShare presentations and so on. For a career developer, creating an impressive and effective layer of digital artifacts is a powerful way of presenting his or her skilled self to the target audience.

Now if we go back to the image representing the candidates screening in the process of competitive selection, we can interpret it as an employer's reading of the available artifacts. This is a process in which the employer scans, processes, and integrates all the layers of information and forms and impression of each candidate. But happens when several equally skilled candidates compete for a job? How do employers make hiring decisions in those situations?

As we saw in the previous lecture, the situation is very similar to one of consumer decision making, in which a consumer needs to make a choice between competing brands. According to consumer behavior researchers, when consumers are facing alternative choices, they combine knowledge with affective feelings about products. To form an overall evaluation or a brand attitude. So, a strong career brand is one that can stand out by reaching the prospective employer on a very deep level, so to speak.

Later in the week and even in more week three, we will examine the process of impression management in more detail. The goal of impression management is to focus and amplify the signal that your career brand is sending to the employer. According to leading authorities on marketing communications, Jack Trout and Al Ries, you have to consider that only a little of your messages is going to get through to the employer [1]. The employers mind can only take in so much information and it blocks out everything that is not important or relevant. Trout and Ries define positioning as what you do to the mind of the prospect. So, your tasks are twofold. First you need to correctly position the product In the mind of a prospect. Second, the signal you are sending must be strong enough.

Now, let's see what you can do for your career brand image to be strong. If you can communicate that you are a genuinely good person, trustworthy, hardworking, and strong values, this is great and absolutely necessary. But cannot be enough to qualify for a highly skilled position. If you can prove that you've got required competencies and skills, you'll add significantly to your brand. Can you adequately support your claim with evidence of your mastery? Can you make your skills and abilities visible?

Now we can do one more step. If you did a good job of creating a solid layer of artifacts to prove and demonstrate your mastery in the field, would it be enough to support your brand? The answer actually depends on the competition in your area. If you are in a rare situation where employers and recruiters are desperately looking for people like you, chances are they will immediately notice and even chase you. But if this is not the case and there is a lot of competition in the area, you will probably need to do more to stand out and promote yourself. How would you do this?

The final layer that you'll need to add to your product is communication various forms, and through a variety of channels. Including interpersonal live communications social media, web presence, referrals and emails. It is though communication that your product your skilled self comes alive and can advocate for you. Without properly arranged and actually working communication channels your skilled self may remain the best kept secret in town.

Let's review what we've discussed so far. The product that you are bringing to the market is your skilled self. It is based on your core self that includes your personal characteristics, personality traits, value and beliefs, and defines who you are. The central element of the skilled self is the unique combination of competencies and skills, the very reason a prospective employer would want to hire you. Each of your skills must be properly documented and supported by artifacts, proving your mastery in the field. Finally, you need to find ways to properly communicate your skilled self to target audiences.

In the following presentations, we'll talk about the use of marketing theory for self-marketing. Some of the topics we'll discuss are what is marketing philosophy? How relevant is it for self-marketing? What is marketing audit, and how can it be used for career branding? What is relationship marketing, network marketing? Is there any use of popular marketing mix models, such as four p and seven c, for self-marketing? I'll see you soon.

Works cited:

[1] Ries, A., & Trout, J. (2001). *Positioning: The Battle for Your Mind.* McGraw-Hill Education.

What Are The Critical Skill Areas for Self-Marketing?

Self-marketing as a skill

By now, you should be able to analyze any competency by breaking it down into corresponding units and elements (critical tasks). Using the same approach, you can think about your self-marketing skills as a CSA (Critical Skill Area). Then, you can break it down to 4-5 key competencies. Please note that there is no "right" way of doing this. How to define key competencies and critical tasks will depend on your particular situation and typical approaches that are used by successful professionals, recruiters, and employers in your field. Also, you should think about other relevant skills (like digital fluency and social media marketing) that you can showcase when presenting your skillset to a potential employer. Here are some of the examples of key competencies, with related elements of competency (critical tasks).

	CSA	**Key competencies (units)**	**Critical tasks**
1	Skills Analysis	1.1. Analyze the job.	Identify the required skillset
		1.2. Analyze your readiness	Conduct an accurate skillset review
2	Job Application	2.1. Use resume to present skills	Skill-based (functional) resume
		2.2. Create USP to stand out	Incorporate USP in the cover letter
		2.3. Respond to selection criteria	Use Selection Criteria Statement
3	Public Profile	3.1. Advertise your skills	Use LinkedIn profile
		3.2. Showcase work samples	Use LinkedIn portfolio feature
4	Communication Skills	4.1. Interviewing skills	Use impression management
		4.2. Persuasion	Use elevator pitch
5	Search for Opportunities	5.1. Resourcefulness	Use Networking, Events
		5.2. Digital self-marketing	Use Social Media, blogging

Using benchmarks and assessment tools for honing self-marketing skills

After you have identified the critical tasks, you should be looking for appropriate benchmarks, best practices, and role models. For example, what would be an exemplary way to use a LinkedIn profile in your case? Do you know how to use it properly? Is there any checklist (=a self-assessment tool) that could tell you that your LinkedIn profile does indeed the job you want it to do? Or, may be, there is a way to obtain a peer or even expert evaluation of your LinkedIn profile. But how would you arrange it?

VIDEO LECTURE: The Skilled Self as a Brand

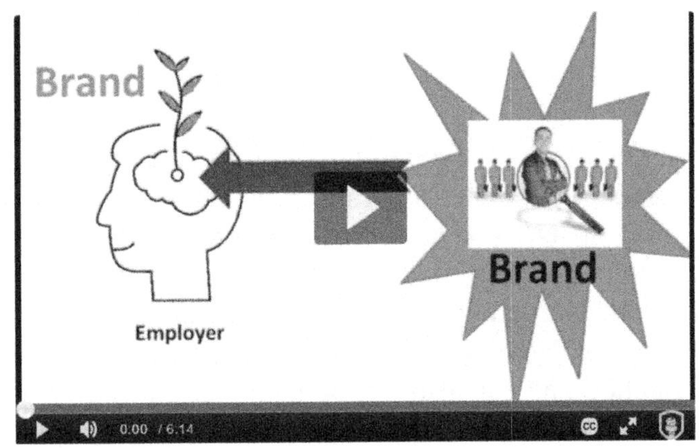

This video presents a professional approach to human branding that you can use to present and promote your skills. The video was filmed for "Career Brand Management" specialization on Coursera .

© The text and slides are prepared by Val Chukhlomin, narration by Amy Giaculli (2016). Image credits: Shuttterstock.com

Please note that in this video we refer to courses on Coursera that follow the same logic as this course, though the sequence of activities is slightly different.

Hello again, in this presentation, we'll discuss the skilled self, as a brand. The theme of personal branding, is the subject matter in week three. We'll demonstrate that this theme goes beyond self-marketing, and touches upon many aspects, of how a person can create, and use social capital, for career development, and personal growth. In this presentation, we'll provide some definitions of brands, and branding in the marketing literature, and see how they can be used in the career development context. Then, we'll invite you to conduct some career branding exercises in the career development lab.

Brands, and branding are popular, and important concepts in marketing literature [1]. In professional services marketing, which is the closest to the career development subset of marketing theory, brand is defined, as the customer's perception of the firm's, or in our case, a skilled professional, capabilities to deliver a high-quality service [2]. The role of the brand, is to communicate, and assure value, guarantee high performance, build trust, create relationship, and provide visibility [3].

In marking literature, you can find many specific terms related to brands, and branding, for example, brand image, brand identity, brand promise, brand personality, brand awareness, brand equity, and many others. The American Marketing Association maintains a website that includes a dictionary of marketing terms [4]. There are some great websites developed by marketing consultants, and companies such as, dotme.com [5]. If you go through branding terminology, you may notice that some of the terms are repetitive, some are only interesting for researchers. The important thing, is that you should not confuse the two ways of dealing with brands. On one hand, brands can be solely viewed on the customer's side, as their perceptions. On the other hand, sellers, or in our case career developers, can actively engage in creating desired images, and transporting them to customers. Finally, in the commercial world, the term brand is often used anonymously with product, but this is not what we meant by brand in the course.

In the world of branding, there's one particular concept that we would like you to become familiar with, it's called brand equity. You may also call it brand capital, in

accounting, they call it goodwill. In a nutshell, brand equity is a tangible outcome of branding, for example, it is the difference between the cost of manufacturing a branded product, and the price that consumers pay for it, or it is the residual value of a branded business, when the total cost of it's material asset is taken out. Please note, that it is the brand equity that makes us understand, that all this talk about perceptions, has real cash value, we'll continue this conversation in a minute.

The idea of self-branding in relation to career growth became popular in the 1990s, particularly after Peters published his book, Brand You [6]. If you google <personal branding>, you'll find plenty of self-help books, and blogs, many of them are actually very good. In this course, we do not want to summarize those resources, as they keep evolving daily. Our goal, is to connect brand building with skill building, and provide a holistic approach to career self-management, with the use of some self-coaching tools.

To understand brands, it's better to think about them, as a means to translate complex messages, and convert them into emotions, and desires, for example, what is Nike, Ferrari, Apple? It is a product, quality of life, a challenge, a dream? In marketing literature, you can read about the brand pyramid that encapsulates the whole spectrum of meanings, and levels of involvement. At this point we'd like to ask you to think about a brand pyramid of your own, what elements would you include in your brand pyramid? In what order? How do you think they're going to promote your professional image, and help you grow, and get a dream job?

To help you begin, let me ask you a few questions, let's begin with an easy one. Do you think that education is relevant, the type of institution you attend, the type of degree you earned? Years ago, a good degree, or any degree, opened doors, it has changed since then, but degrees still do matter. This is information that can be easily communicated in a resume, if it is important for the employer that you graduated from, say Caltech, then they may recall it, and think about you, as a Caltech guy, if they do then you know that your brand exists, at least they can recall it.

What's next? The next question is about your functional skills. Is there anything that you can demonstrate in a uniquely memorable way? Something that can help you stand out, even if all other candidates have comparable skills? This is where a well-chosen artifact can create a point of difference. The next question is about your personality, of course many job candidates can be creative, resilient, and adaptive, but try to prove it in an unusual, and emotional way, and create a more powerful impression.

Now, this is time to ask you the most important question, are you ready? What do you think is a tangible outcome of career branding? How can you measure it? The thing is, that if you can identify, pinpoint, and measure the outcome of career branding, then you can manage it, and use it for your career success. To measure tangible outcomes of career branding, it's logical to use the concept of brand equity. We can define a person's career brand equity, as the surplus, and his or her evaluation by employers, and colleagues caused by career branding activities. You may think about it this way, if there are two job candidates, Peter and Paul, with more, or less equivalent functional skills, but one of them,

Peter, has designed a more powerful professional image, his present job market value is going to be higher, than the one of Paul. To explore this approach in more detail, we invite you to the career development lab, see you there.

Works cited:

[1] Keller, K.L. (2012). *Strategic Brand Management.* 4th ed. Pearson.
[2] Shultz, M., & Doerr, J.E. (2013). *Professional Services Marketing.* 2nd ed. Wiley.
[3] Chernatony L (2006). *From Brand Vision to Brand Evaluation.* 2nd ed. Butterworth-Heinemann.
[4] American Marketing Association. https://www.ama.org
[5] Introducing DotMe. Https://estuous.com/dotme
[6] Peters, T. (1999). *Brand You 50.* Knopf.

Presenting your personal brand to the world

You public (professional) profile

What you do in your Skills Lab is your private business and you probably do not need to share it with anyone except a mentor, career coach, or a trusted peer reviewer. But how do you tell the world that you have transformed into a skilled professional? For this purpose, you will need to create a public (professional) profile. Your public profile is a carefully selected collection of artifacts that is supposed to best represent your professional self for external audiences. An old-age, traditional way to create a public profile is to use a resume, a CV, a bio sketch, a professional publication, a newspaper article about you, or a reference letter. In the digital era, a public profile is created with the use of LinkedIn, social media, websites and blogging, and other means that can be used to communicate and showcase your skills. So, what is your public profile and what do you want it to be?

Self-marketing communications mix

Your career brand is your professional image in the eyes of your colleagues and potential employers. As you can learn from the discipline of marketing, brands can be successfully managed. Creating an informative and powerful public profile is a very important step for managing your career brand. Also, it is not a one-time activity, as your skills portfolio and the level of expertise will be growing over time. In terms of the most relevant marketing approach for building an effective public profile, you can build on the concept of service marketing communications mix (see the 7P Framework in the text and assigned readings).

Marketing communications mix includes several components and activities that help potential customers learn about the brand and its unique characteristics, relate them to their needs, and eventually come to a buying decision. The components and activities include advertising, direct marketing, personal selling, sales promotion, and PR. The same approach can be used for self-marketing, where a public profile takes the place of advertising. The goals of advertising are to not just make a potential buyer aware of the brand but to also create interest and desire to act. Do you think your public profile should serve the same goals? If yes, how this can be achieved?

Your LinkedIn account

LinkedIn (www.linkedin.com) is one of the most popular tools for creating a professional public profile. It combines a resume, a career portfolio (with work samples), and a platform for peer reviewing and networking. Also, the LinkedIn Resume Assistant plugin, which is a new addition to MS Word, is very helpful in identifying key competencies and critical tasks.

In this course we assume that you have already created a LinkedIn profile. Does it serve its goal and what the goal is? What is the advertising message that your LinkedIn profile is supposed to carry? How do you think other people do it? Are you aware of any exemplary LinkedIn profiles in your professional field? What makes them exemplary? Can you think of an assessment rubric for a LinkedIn portfolio? Can you create a rubric to use for your LinkedIn profile? How would you rate yourself? How do you think you can improve?

Career portfolio

As mentioned earlier, a career portfolio is a collection of your work samples to be presented to potential employers for demonstrating your mastery of skills. It can be actual samples or observations of your work made by experts, supervisors, and peers. Also, it can be a collection of certifications and badges. Having samples is helpful for demonstrating your mastery but you may not be allowed to showcase the actual work you have done for other employers. One way of demonstrating your skills is to use a self-talk in the form of a slide or video presentation. You may find it useful to store it in a publicly available platform (like, "YouTube" or "SlideShare") and reference on your LinkedIn account.

The use of social media

Social media are now universally used for communication and self-promotion; we suggest that you discuss and practice the use of social media for self-marketing in Module 5. In addition, make sure that you find and read relevant scholarly sources, as this topic is being heavily researched. In particular, we suggest that you read the following articles. Jose van Dijck (2013) in his article discussed the problem of online identity formation comparing Facebook and LinkedIn. The use of LinkedIn for accounting and business students is discussed in a brief article by W. David Albrecht (2011). The effects of LinkedIn on deception in resumes are discussed in an article by Jamie Guillory and Jeffrey Hancock (2012).

Your Active Behaviors: A Powerful Elevator Pitch

Active behaviors

One can only achieve positive career outcomes through active behaviors, such as job market scanning, new job applications, promotion requests, skill building, career skills development, and personal skills development for career growth and self-realization. In a limited time that working adults have for their continuing education and professional development, they often neglect investing into developing their career building skills – probably because those skills are typically not explicitly mentioned in job advertisements. In this course we advocate for taking career development skills more seriously; for example, by paying attention to self-marketing skills. In this Module, we will explore how you can use a powerful self-marketing communication tool known as "Elevator Pitch" to promote your USP for the position you specified in Module 2.

What is Elevator Pitch?

In the assignment 5, we will ask you to conduct a thorough research on elevator pitch as a marketing communication strategy. You will also need to analyze it as a skill, find out benchmarks and assessment tools, and come up with a message map for your USP, peer-assessment strategy, and a self-assessment tool. Then, you will need to flex your digital muscles, create and record a powerful pitch, and get it peer reviewed.

Your Elevator Pitch as a self-administered training intervention

It may happen that you are already a highly qualified elevator pitcher but what we have learned is that most students are usually not. Even more, many people do not feel comfortable to either speaking publicly, or recording and showcasing themselves, or speaking about own skills. But in a skill-based, competitive job environment, having this skill is a must. So, what we will do is to arrange a self-administered training intervention in a safe and trusted environment. As you are now familiar with your small group and you are not in a competitive situation, we invite you to work collectively on this, not very easy task, and help yourself and each other. In the end, you should be able to produce a well-written, persuasive, energetic, and well-recorded pitch introducing your USP for the position in Module 2. We also expect that you will peer review two-three other people presentations and provide a friendly, but honest and helpful developmental feedback. The intended outcome of this activity is that you will be able to better: 1) analyze your skillset; 2) connect it to your personal strengths and abilities; 3) relate to the prospective employer's interest; 4) express it succinctly and persuasively.

A note on presentation skills

It is likely that presentation skills are one of the critical skills that are included into your Dashboard. You may use your presentation for a) self-assessing your skill; b) soliciting feedback from your peers. For any of these purposes, you will need a rubric. Actually, it's good to have a valid presentation skills rubric in your personal lab anyway. To find one, you may want to google <presentation skills rubric>.

References

- Albrecht, D., W. (2011). LinkedIn for Accounting and Business Students. *American Journal of Business Education, 4(10),* 39-42.

- Dijck, J. (2013). 'You have one identity': performing the self on Facebook and LinkedIn, *Media, Culture & Society, 35(2)*, 199-215.

- Guillory, J., and Hancock, J. (2012). The effects of LinkedIn on deception in resumes. *Cyberpsychology, Behavior and Social Networking, 15(3),* 135-140. DOI: 10.1089/cyber.2011.0389.

Discussion D5: Using social media marketing for self-promotion

How to market yourself professionally? Can you use proven business strategy methods and tools (for example, marketing communication mix, or unique selling proposition, or professional services marketing, or digital marketing strategies) for self-marketing and personal branding? How can you use social media marketing for self-promotion?

In your response, please identify the important concepts, theories, or ideas that you have learned regarding self-promotion through social media marketing.

Why do you think these concepts, theories, or ideas are important? How would you apply what you have learned in this and other marketing courses to successfully promote yourself using social media marketing? Please give a few examples.

Also, what question(s) has your learning of self-promotion through social media marketing raised for you? What are you still wondering about?

Module M6:

Effective Self-Regulation for SMARTER Outcomes

Overview

The goal of the Module is to learn how to effectively set and achieve your skill-building and self-promotional goals.

In the Module, you will synthesize all self-management and self-marketing methods and techniques that we have learned in the course for effective self-programming and reaching your skill-building goals. You will begin by examining learning theories of self-directed learning, active regulation, goal setting, and feedback-seeking behavior. As a practical application, you will engage in peer reviewing of student elevator pitch presentations prepared in the previous Module. Then, you will review a popular SMART and SMARTER goals technique and examine ways of utilizing it for guiding your skill-building activities. After that, you will focus on developing your data-driven, evidence-based, and results-oriented skill-building plan (PDP) and planning self-administered training interventions.

Module Learning Objectives:

M6-1	Examine learning theories of self-directed learning, active regulation, goal setting, and feedback-seeking behavior.	**R6**
M6-2	Examine peer review techniques and discuss the usefulness of feedback seeking behaviors.	**D6**
M6-3	Critically review a popular SMART goals technique and examine ways of utilizing it for guiding your skill-building activities to maximize your likely total skillset score in a competitive job selection context.	**R6, CPW6**
M6-4	Develop a data-driven, evidence-based, and results-oriented skill-building plan (SBP).	**A6**
M6-5	Plan a series of self-administered training interventions and active behaviors to achieve your skill-building and career growth goals.	**A6**

On S.M.A.R.T. and S.M.A.R.T.E.R. goals

You have probably heard of the recommendation to use S.M.A.R.T. goals. Or maybe you are familiar with the implementation of this concept in the business planning context. Like many other tools, S.M.A.R.T goals are often oversimplified or misunderstood. For example, consider the following dialog:

- *Are your goals S.M.A.R.T?*
- *Yes, of course, my goals are always smart, because I am a smart person!*

Does it sound familiar?

Meanwhile, this concept, if properly used, can be instrumental and very powerful for skills development. Before discussing it in more detail, let's clarify the original meaning of the concept.

S.M.A.R.T. is a mnemonic acronym that was introduced by business strategists in the 1980s. S.M.A.R.T stands for "Specific", "Measurable", "Achievable", "Relevant", and "Time-Bound". The framework was initially meant to provide guidance for setting goals in the project management context. In the 1990s, the S.M.A.R.T. goals framework was further adjusted by adding E. ("Evaluate") and R. ("Re-adjust") components to close the loop in accordance with the systems theory recommendation. Now, goals become dynamic, adjustable, and they better connect with the overall strategy. The resultant S.M.A.R.T.E.R. goals framework is highly regarded in the business literature.

The main idea behind S.M.A.R.T.E.R. goals is that to effectively execute a strategy, the company's managers need to establish concrete milestones. By accomplishing them one by one even a very complex strategy can be successfully and timely executed. The same logic is perfectly applicable for self-strategy. That's why the concept of S.M.A.R.T.E.R. goals were enthusiastically adopted for use in the professional development context. By now, it is well supported by research that people in their work and personal life tend to achieve better results if they can translate them into specific, measurable, and achievable goals.

The problem with the implementation of S.M.A.R.T.E.R goals in the personal development domain is that it is not clear how to formulate them for a concrete person in a concrete situation. That's why we often look for help from trainers, coaches, or mentors. Think about it: in companies, there are MBA-trained strategic planners that use well-designed procedures to develop competitive strategies and to translate them into S.M.A.R.T.E.R. goals. They use many sophisticated tools including balance scorecards. They do it full-time and are paid for that. The question is how an ordinary person could possibly design a sequence of steps to achieve a competitive advantage in the labor market, especially in real time, with no professional training, and tons of other things to deal with or think about.

This is where the individual skills management methodology that we use in this course can be helpful. By design, the model is aimed at gaining a competitive edge in the job market. It helps translate the idea of being competitive into realistic scores, targets, and the steps to reach the targets.

The above text is adapted from: Chukhlomin, V. (2018). *How to Get Skilled.* Upward Mobility Books, Saratoga Springs, NY. To learn more about S.M.A.R.T. goals, you should start here:

- Doran, G. T. (1981). There's a S.M.A.R.T. Way to Write Management's Goals and Objectives. *Management Review*, 70 (11), pp. 35–36.

Active regulation

The theory behind establishing work-related SMARTER goals is called goal setting (see Locke and Latham in the readings). The idea of goal-setting and active regulation is to thoroughly review your workplace situation and the required skillset, then evaluate your existing skillset against the relevant benchmark, identify strengths, parities, and weaknesses, and after that design and execute a very concrete and detailed plan for improvement. The very handy thing is that in Modules 3-4 you have already learned most of it. Now, you need to go back to the CSD tool to find out how it can used for establishing and monitoring your SMARTER goals.

To learn more about goal setting, we recommend using the following source:

- Locke, E., & Latham, G.P. (Eds.) (2013). *New Developments in Goal Setting and Task Performance*. New York, Routledge.

Using your CSD (Critical Skills Dashboard) for setting concrete, quantifiable goals

In your CSD (Module 4) review the areas labelled yellow and red where some significant (or major) improvements are required in order you can get a higher T.S.S. (total skillset score). This is how it may look like:

	Critical Task	Description of problems: I scored low in (.) because of (.)
1.2.1	Analytical reports	- Weak theoretical analysis (assumptions, models, narrative);
3.1.1.	Advanced MS Excel skills	- Do not use VBA variables and writing macros; - Cannot work with Pivot tables.

The important thing is to specify in detail what the problem is, what is your current level and what a desired level would be (for example, you may find out that if you were at least an intermediate level specialist in Advanced MS Excel, then your overall T.S.S, for the position would be, say, 75% instead of current 58%). This information should be enough to provide you with S.M.A.R.T.E.R. goals for your Skill-Building Plan.

Your skill-building activity as a self-administered training intervention

When you decide to engage in self-initiated, skill-building activities, it is helpful to think about it as a self-administered training intervention where you play the roles of both the athlete and the coach. As an athlete, you keep tirelessly training. As a coach, you are responsible for setting goals and monitoring the progress. Also, you should be thinking about how to instill confidence, provide support and give constructive feedback, and provide training evaluation in the end. Is it at all possible? How do other people do it? Is there any theory behind it that I can use? This is where you may probably want to know more about self-regulated learning (SRL) and self-directed learning (SDL) and test your SDL skills.

Self-directed learning skills

Self-directed learning (SDL) skills

Self-directed learning (SDL) is the foundational concept of this course. In Module 2 content guides you were introduced to the theme of self-regulated and self-directed learning. Now it's time to reflect and self-assess your SDL skills and perhaps add them to your CSA Profile and Dashboard and Professional Development (Skill-Building) Plan.

More on SDL skills

In the period of rapid changes, SDL skills are among the most important skills; in order to stay current and to be competitive, one needs to know how to acquire new knowledge and skills and do it efficiently. At this point, we suggest that you read a few more articles on the topic. In 'Teach me How to Learn", Gregory Francom (2010) provided a brief review of literature on SDL and describes four main principles that can be derived from the literature. A previously quoted article by Andrea Ellinger (2004) provides detailed descriptions of SDL processes and implications for the workplace. Chris Patterson, Dauna Crooks and Ola Linyk-Child (2002) reported of an academic program in Canada where SDL skills and competencies were taught as part of the curriculum and described elements of competency and related rubrics for assessment/self-assessment.

Constructive feedback

Receiving an objective, motivating, accurate and constructive feedback is one of the cornerstones of self-regulated learning and skills development. In Discussion 6 we suggest that you provide feedback to your peers and receive feedback from them and discuss related issues.

Transformative learning

Developing SDL skills results in a major shift in the learner's attitudes and behaviors; this is captured and described by transformative learning theory. The best way to familiarize with this theory is to study the seminal article of Jack Mesirow (2000) on transformative learning.

Professional Development (Skill-Building) Plan

Download the template, develop the plan and submit it in the designated area.

Self-Audit

Assignment 7 is designed as a post-test self-audit. Please respond to the questions and provide your reflection.

What Can We Learn from Business Strategy?

From external analysis and SWOT to formulating and implementing strategies

Most organizations routinely do strategic planning, nevertheless only some of them succeed and some do not. One of the most difficult problems is how to scan the external environment correctly and come up with meaningful results; another problem is how to predict the future and prepare for that by developing necessary skills in advance. Suppose that one has got a kind of a "crystal ball" to see the future and has developed an excellent strategic plan to excel in that future. But how can they implement and sustain the strategy? Change is not easy; organizations are known to be subject of so called "path dependence" and routinely fail to implement strategies of change. So do individuals. We suggest that you discuss related issues in Discussion D6.

Now, how can we use proven business strategy methods and tools (for example, TOWS analysis or a balanced scoring card) for self-management, and why should we? You may start by discussing advantages of using business strategy for an organization (take a look at the following website: http://www.s-m-i.net/pdf/Business%20strategy%20intro.pdf or just google <advantages of using business strategy>). Then, read some suggestions by HR consultants (google <personal balanced score card>). Do you think that this kind of an effort makes sense? What are the advantages? Any associated problems? Can it be sustainable? In the long run? How?

A personal balanced scoring card

To implement a strategy, organizations oftentimes use an instrument called "a balanced scoring card". As stated by the Balanced Scorecard Institute,

> *The balanced scorecard is a strategic planning and management system that is used extensively in business and industry, government, and nonprofit organizations worldwide to align business activities to the vision and strategy of the organization, improve internal and external communications, and monitor organization performance against strategic goals. It was originated by Drs. Robert Kaplan (Harvard Business School) and David Norton as a performance measurement framework that added strategic non-financial performance measures to traditional financial metrics to give managers and executives a more 'balanced' view of organizational performance. While the phrase balanced scorecard was coined in the early 1990s, the roots of the this type of approach are deep, and include the pioneering work of General Electric on performance measurement reporting in the 1950's and the work of French process engineers (who created the Tableau de Bord – literally, a "dashboard" of performance measures) in the early part of the 20th century.*

Some career management consultants suggested using the concept for self-management. You may find it useful to get familiar with the work of Hubert Rampersad, particularly, the idea of using a personal balanced scorecard. A similar approach to personal balanced scoring card is presented in a document created by Elena Salazar.

Closing the loop: revising goals and skills

One of the important elements of corporate strategy-making is to continuously monitor the environment and if necessary, revise goals and strategies. A similar approach can be taken for self-management based on the data presented in the Dashboard.

References

- Ellinger, A. (2004). The Concept of Self-Directed Learning and Its Implications for Human Resource Development. *Advances in Developing Human Resources, 6(2),* 158-177. DOI: 10.1177/1523422304263327.
- Francom, G. M. (2011). Teach me how to learn: Principles for fostering students' self-directed learning skills. *International Journal of Self-Directed Learning, 7*(1), 29-44.
- Mezirow, J. (2000). *Learning as Transformation: Critical Perspectives on a Theory in Progress*. San Francisco: Jossey Bass.
- Patterson, C., Crooks, D., and Linyk-Child, O. (2002). A New Perspective on Competencies for Self-Directed Learning. *Journal of Nursing Education, 41(1)*, 25-31.

Discussion D6: Constructive feedback and the power of peer review (Post your YOU TUBE link here!)

One of the ways in which we internalize the characteristics of quality work is by evaluating the work of our peers. For this Module's discussion you will assess your colleagues' presentations from Module 5 and provide constructive feedback (Please post your You Tube link for your Elevator Pitch from Module 5 to this discussion).

You must provide feedback to at least three different colleagues and your feedback to your colleague must address the following questions:

1. What aspects of their work were successful, and why?
2. What aspects of their work are less successful, and why?
3. How could your colleague improve this particular piece of work?
4. How could your colleague do more successful work in future?

When discussing your peers' work, use a rubric.

Module M7:

Reflection and Reinforcement: Career Self-Management Workflow

Overview

This is a very short, one day Module. The goal of the Module is to provide you with an opportunity to review your progress in the course; also, to think about how to sustain your career building effort in the future. In Assignment 7, you will review the results, reflect on your career competencies, and evaluate your level of self-confidence in implementing the methods and techniques that you have learned in the course. Then, we will invite you to think about the ongoing self-coaching. In particular, we will propose a technique that may be helpful for you to organize and maintain an effective career self-management workflow in the future.

Module Learning Objectives:

M7-1	Review your progress in the course, reflect on your career competencies, and evaluate your level of self-confidence in implementing the methods and techniques that you have learned in the course.	**A7**
M7-2	Review self-coaching techniques in light of the learning theories and career self-management methodologies examined in the course.	**R7**
M7-3	Identify and examine information technologies that can be used to effectively organize and maintain your career self-management workflow.	**CPW7**

VIDEO LECTURE: Career Self-Management Information System

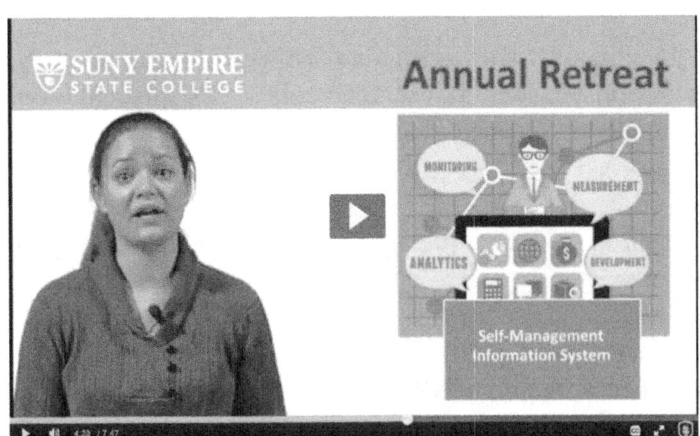

This video presents a professional approach to organizing your career self-management workflow that you can use for ongoing career development. The video was filmed for "Career Brand Management" specialization on Coursera in 2016.

© The text and slides are prepared by Val Chukhlomin, narration by Amy Giaculli (2016). Image credits: Shuttterstock.com

Please note that in this video we refer to courses on Coursera that follow the same logic as this course, though the sequence of activities is slightly different.

Hello again! Today's theme is the self-audit. This is where we would like to ask you to collect and review all results of your self-auditing exercises from the entire specialization. You did quite a lot of them. Here's a list. Please make sure that you have them all completed.

In course 1, you were able to identify your portable skills portfolio, career self-management competencies and gaps, personality traits, self-controls and self-directed learning skills, as well as your career goals and future work self. In course two, you worked on your self-assessment skills, skill building skills, SWOT analysis and a 360-degree self-assessment. In course 3, you conducted a self-marketing audit.

When you go on a retreat next year, you'll probably want to repeat at least some of the self-auditing exercises. To do so, there's no need to retake all three courses in specialization but you may still benefit from reviewing the career development lab activities and the content videos in those courses before conducting self-audits. This time, we assume that you have just completed all of the exercises and courses one, two, and three, and have your self-auditing results ready for review. In this case, the next step will be to move to day three of the retreat which is dedicated to making sense of the self-audit and figuring out where you are supposed to engage in strategic planning for the year to come.

But before you move to day three, we'd like to take some time to review the effectiveness of your self-developmental and self-promotional work. There are three particular aspects of it that we would like to focus on in this module. These aspects are the use of your self-management information system, the effectiveness of peer review assessment and peer feedback, and your mastery in documenting your skills.

You may ask yourself why you need this. How are these related to self-audits? Here's our rationale. First, your self-management information system. You may think about it as a self-audit of your organizational skills. This is a very important and highly practical application of self-management theory because if you cannot organize and keep track of your activities, you can hardly be in control of your self-development to work. We did talk about the need to setup an effective self-management information system and the specialization and provide it some recommendations. Now, is the time to review it and share your observations.

We also added a lecture on peer review, because peer assessment is often the only available feedback that a career developer can get in real time. How could we make it useful, valuable, and functional? We covered this subject in some detail in course two, when we discussed self-assessment. But it makes sense to talk more about it during the retreat where you can actually work with your cohort in real time.

Finally, we included a lecture and an assignment devoted to developing a digital artifact during the retreat because by engaging in a highly practical application of your self-developmental work, you can see that these tools actually work. If you do your self-audits correctly, you will see how you can better develop and articulate your marketable skills.

Now, let's go back to your self-management information system. To begin, what is a self-management information system? Why does one need it? And how does one organize it scientifically? In a way, most people have a self-management information system in a form of some notes, records, a diary, etc. Of course, in the digital age, these notes become digitized and stored. To figure out how to use the power of information technology to help solve out developmental work, we can take a look at how companies used the information system to perform strategic management, marketing or human resource development functions.

In the business world, management information systems are very heavily used and are becoming highly specialized. Even ten years ago, one could easily get by with learning the foundation of management information systems. These days, there are highly specialized information system in practically every functional area of business including accounting, information systems, human resource information systems, marketing information systems, and so on. You may ask rather you should wait until a new scientific self-management information system appears on the market. We touch on the subject in course two where we contemplated the power of personal analytics and discussed the quantified self-movement. In a nutshell, it's not easy to develop a unified system that serves everyone regardless of their individual differences. But we'll certainly see more of it in the future. In the meantime, in the specialization, we chose to only discuss the principles of self-management information systems and how they can be used by career developers in their everyday lives.

A self-management information system is simply a way to organize your personal records so as to allow you to monitor your self-developmental work. It can be done in an old-fashioned paper-based form. Also, it can be partially or fully digitized. To be practical, it must allow easy access entering and retrieving of data. Ideally, it should allow you to analyze the data use self-developmental or self-coaching tools and present results in a meaningful and useful way. For example, by generating selection criteria statements, resumes, personal profiles, etc. In course one, we recommended a very simple approach to building your self-management information system by creating three folders on your computer or on the cloud, which include materials designated as input, processing, and output.

Input included external materials like job advertisings, resources, good examples, assessment and self-assessment tools, peer reviews, etc. Processing included internally generated materials like your analysis, self-audits, self-assessments, etc. And output, included the documents that you prepare for sharing and external use such as job applications, websites, public profiles, professional development plans, and the like.

At this point, we'd like to ask you about your experience in setting up your self-management information system. Was it easy? How did you do it? How did you further organize your folders? Was it useful for self-organization?

The next question is, what do you do with it? Did you set it up and forget it? How many self-audits did you do? Where do you record the results? Did you link them to outputs? Finally, what are your thoughts about improving and further customizing it for your needs? If you deal with the information systems in any specialized field what would you recommend based on your professional experience?

Conducting an audit of your self-management information system is part of the comprehensive self-audit. Its goal is to increase the effectiveness of self-developmental work. In addition to the questions that we just asked you, you may also consider the overall usefulness of the system for your ongoing professional development. Realistically, it may be very hard to sustain this kind of effort during the year. It's like a New Year's resolution. It's better not to go to the gym in early January, because that's usually gets too crowded there, for a little while. It may be important to setup very realistic expectations about using your self-management information system during the year. Enjoy!

Reflecting and Moving Forward

In the end of the course it is a good idea to think about your career self-management strategy in general and some tactical ways of implementing it. For example, how would you answer the following questions:

1. Have you decided about your career growth scenarios?
2. Did you schedule your active behaviors?
3. Do you have a skill-building plan?
4. Do you have a self-marketing & personal branding plan?
5. How are you going to organize your career self-management workflow?

Your next step: How to organize an effective Career Self-Management Workflow

Module 7 is a bonus part of the course where we share some ideas about how to incorporate career self-management in your daily routines. For example, you may want to explore a new tool, OneNote CSM Workbook. You can download it in the course. You will see that this is the same Workbook that you are using in the course (Figure 4). But it is done in a free Microsoft software called OneNote. OneNote is actually an electronic journal and a diary. You can use it as an ABC portfolio as discussed earlier. You can use it as a career fitness diary following the logic we presented in this course. It is all in one place, accessible on your phone/tablet and integrated with other Microsoft software.

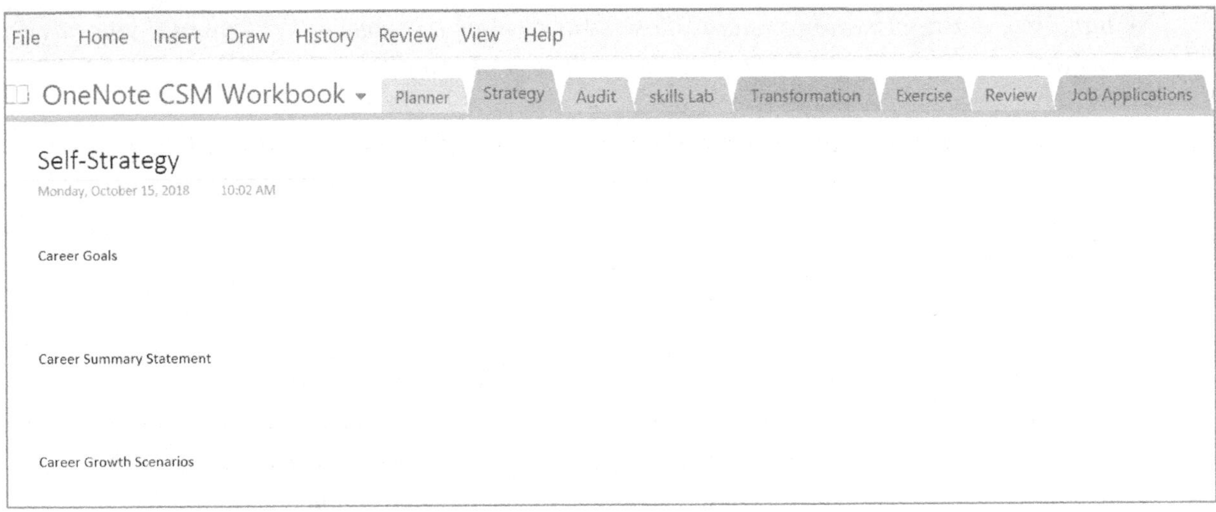

Figure 4: OneNote Career Self-Management Workbook

Instructional Materials and Templates

Career Self-Management e-Portfolio and Learning Journal Workbook

Career Self-Management E-Portfolio & Workbook

Student:		ID Number (optional)	
Area of Studies		Concentration	
Term, year		Instructor	

Contents:

Module	Strategy ¦ Audit ¦ Skills Lab	Transformation, Exercises (Tools)	Pages
M1	Occupational Area. Career Summary Statement. Immediate and long-term Career Goals. Career Growth Scenarios. Career Development Resources and Tools. Career Building Skills.	Resume. LinkedIn or Facebook account (optional)	
M2	Future Work Self. Professional, Generic (Transferable), and Personal Skills, Abilities & Attributes. Personal (Skill-Based) SWOT Analysis. Building on strengths, eliminating weaknesses.	Personal SWOT Analysis. Selection Criteria Statement	
M3	CSA (Critical Skill Areas). Key Competencies (=Units of Competency). Elements of Competency. Critical Tasks. Job-Specific Skillset. Mastery Performance: Role Models, Best Practices, Standards, Benchmarks. Skills Assessment. Evidence of Mastery. Self-Assessment.	Critical Skills Assessment Tool (CSAT). Personal VRIO Analysis.	
M4	Critical Skills Dashboard (CSD). Total Skillset Score (TSS). Accuracy of Assessment. Feedback Seeking: Expert and Peer-Assessment. Personal SWOT Re-Evaluation: Competitive Advantages, Parities, and Skill Gaps. Skillset Review Summary.	CSD+TSS; Skillset Review Summary. Personal Balanced Score Card (optional)	
M5	Personal (Career) Brand. Skilled (Professional) Self. USP. Self-Marketing Skills (the 7P Framework). Self-Marketing KSA. ABC Portfolio. Public Profile. Self-Marketing Communication Mix. Career Portfolio. Active Behavior: Elevator Pitch. Self-Administered Training Intervention. Self-Marketing and Personal Branding Strategy/Plan.(SMP). Functional Resume. LinkedIn (optional).	SMPB Plan: Elevator Pitch: Functional Resume. LinkedIn updated (optional)	
M6	Active Behaviors. Feedback Seeking: Peer Review. Goal Setting: S.M.A.R.T. and S.M.A.R.T.E.R. goals. Active Regulation. The Use of CSD for Setting and Monitoring Skill-Building Goals. Skill-Building Plan (SBP). Training Interventions. Self-Directed Learning (SDL). Self-Confidence and Self-Efficacy.	SMARTER goals: Skill-Building Plan (SBP)	
M7	Career Building Skills (revisited). Career Fitness. Career Self-Management Workflow. Next steps and additional tools.	OneNote CPW; JAFAR®	

Attachments (to be submitted with your Workbook file):

- ✓ Module 1: Resume
- ✓ Module 5: Functional Resume. LinkedIn (optional)

Module 1: Career Self-Management: Your Personal Strategy for Career Success

Planner	**Strategy**	**Audit**	Skills **Lab**	**Transformation**	**Exercise**	**Review**

Module 1 Tasks:

1. **Readings R1.** You should begin this Module by reading the Content Guide, the textbook, and recommended articles.
2. **Discussion D1.** Post your answer, read other posts, and respond to at least two people.
3. **Workbook (CPW1).** Set up your Workbook file. It is mandatory that you use the provided MS Word template. In Module 1, you will need to collect and enter the required information in the following sections of the Workbook (see instructions below):
   - **Strategy.**
   - **Audit.**

- **Review:** Add to KnowledgeBase and Self-Reflection in CPW1.

4. **Assignments.** Complete the Module by working on Assignment A1.

Planner	**Strategy**	**Audit**	Skills **Lab**	**Transformation**	**Exercise**	**Review**

Your Occupational Area Snapshot:

<How would you describe a broad occupational area of your expertise/interest? Explain briefly by providing examples of jobs, typical job titles, required education, certifications>

My Occupational Area:

Your Career (Resume) Summary Statement

<How do you see yourself as a successful job candidate? Explain briefly by highlighting your accomplishments and personal strengths.> Examples

My Career Summary Statement:

Your Career Goals

< Briefly describe here your career goals, both immediate and long-term (2-3 paragraphs).> Examples.

My Career Goals:

1.

2.

3.

Your Career Growth Scenarios

< Using Career Growth Matrix in the textbook (pp 29-30), identify and briefly describe four career growth scenarios as you see fit in your situation.>

My Career Growth Scenarios:

1.

2.

3.

4.

Planner	Strategy	**Audit**	Skills Lab	Transformation	Exercise	Review

Your Career Development Resources and Tools

< Are you aware of any useful resources or tools, for example, software applications, websites, that can be useful for career development and skill-building? List and briefly describe your career development resources and tools. >

My Career Development Resources and Tools:

1.

2.

3.

4.

Your Career Building (=Career Self-Management) Skills

< List and briefly describe your career-building (career self-management) skills.>

My Career Self-Management Skills:

1.

2.

3.

4.

5.

Planner	Strategy	Audit	Skills Lab	Transformation	Exercise	Review

Knowledgebase: Your Learning Resources

<Add here 2-3 NEW resources (books, articles, websites, blogs etc.) that you have learned about during the course. Please do not include either the course textbook, or resources cited in the textbook.>

1.

2.

3.

Reflective Notes

<Explain in 2-3 paragraphs the main topics and ideas discussed in this Module. What have you learned? Do not cite the textbook here, use your own words.>

My Notes:

CPW-1 SUBMISSION:

When finished, submit the Career Self-Management E-Portfolio & Workbook file in the designated box. Please do not cut and paste; just keep working in the Workbook continuously and every time submit the entire Workbook file (this is because in every Module I will need to see all your work that you have done in Workbook during the course). Do not forget to complete and attach your Resume as a separate file. Due date: End of Module 1.

Module 2: Individual Skills Management

Planner	Strategy	Audit	Skills Lab	Transformation	Exercise	Review

Module 2 Tasks:

1. **Readings R2/Videos C2.** Start by reading the text, content guides, and assigned articles.
2. **CPW2.** Then, you should move to Strategy and Audit sections in the Workbook.
   - **Strategy**
   - **Audit.**
3. **Discussion D2.** Post your answer, read other posts and respond to at least two people.
4. **Assignments.** This Module assignment has two parts and it may take quite some time for you to complete. You should not leave it until the last moment. This is the KEY EXERCISE for the entire course. The better you do it, the more useful for you the course is going to be.
5. **CPW2.** To complete the Module, please add to the K-Base and Reflective Notes.
   - **Review: KnowledgeBase**
   - **Review: Self-Reflection.**

Planner	Strategy	Audit	Skills Lab	Transformation	Exercise	Review

Your Future Work Self

< Briefly describe here how you see your career in one, three, and five years from now. Please focus on your skills and explain how your progress in attaining the skills will help you accomplish your career goals.>

My Future Work Self:

Planner	Strategy	Audit	Skills Lab	Transformation	Exercise	Review

Your Professional Skills

<List here your professional skills (you can find definitions of professional skills in Module 2 Content Guides/resources).>

My Professional Skills:

1.

2.

3.

4.

5.

6.

Your Generic (transferable) Skills

<List here your generic skills (you can find definitions of generic skills in Module 2 Content Guides/resources).>

My Generic (Transferable) Skills:

1.

2.

3.

4.

5.

6.

Your Personal Skills, Abilities, and Attributes

< Describe here your personal characteristics, qualities, abilities, and traits that you think are transferable to your current or future jobs.> Examples.

My Personal Skills and Abilities:

1.

2.

3.

4.

5.

6.

Your Personal, Skill-Based SWOT Analysis

< In Discussion 2, you analyzed your skills trying to derive strengths and weaknesses in light of various environmental threats and opportunities. Please highlight your main findings here.>

My Strengths:

My Weaknesses:

My Threats:

My Opportunities:

<Please explain how the above information is helpful for crafting your personal strategy>.

When working on your career development strategy, you should build on strengths and eliminate weaknesses:

	Threats	Opportunities
Strengths	<explain here how your strengths will help mitigating the threats>	<explain here how your strengths will help taking advantage of the opportunities>
Weaknesses	<explain here how your weaknesses may create vulnerabilities in light of the emerging threats and what can be done to eliminate them>	<explain here how your weaknesses may prevent taking advantage of the emerging opportunities and what can be done to eliminate them>

Planner	Strategy	Audit	Skills Lab	Transformation	Exercise	Review

Selection Criteria Statement

<One can only achieve positive career outcomes through active behaviors, such as job market scanning or a new job application. As an exercise, you will be working on Assignments A2-1 and A2-2 in this Module. You may download the assignment template now and begin working on it by following the instructions.>

Planner	Strategy	Audit	Skills Lab	Transformation	Exercise	Review

Knowledgebase: My Learning Resources

<Add here 3-4 NEW resources (books, articles, websites, blogs etc.) that are useful for your ongoing professional development. Please do not include either the course textbook, or resources cited in the textbook.>

1.

2.

3.

4.

Reflective Notes

<Explain in 2-3 paragraphs the main topics and ideas discussed in this Module. What have you learned? Do not cite the textbook here, use your own words.>

My Notes:

CPW-2 SUBMISSION:

When finished, submit the Career Self-Management E-Portfolio & Workbook file in the designated box. Please do not cut and paste; just keep working in the Workbook continuously and every time submit the entire Workbook file. Due date: see Course Schedule.

Module 3: Self-Audit and Skills Analysis

Planner	Strategy	Audit	Skills Lab	Transformation	Exercise	Review

<u>**Module 3 Tasks:**</u>

1. **Readings R3/Videos C3.** Start by reading the text, content guides, and assigned articles.
2. **Discussion D3.** Then, we want you to reflect on your Assignment A2 in Discussion D3.
3. **CPW3.** After that you should move to the Audit and Skills Lab in the Workbook.
- **Audit.**
- **Skills Lab**
4. **Tool: CSAT.** Use the results of your skills assessment in CPW3 to populate the CSAT.
5. **Assignments A3.** The tasks are designed to analyze the process of self- assessment.
6. **CPW3.** To complete the Module, please add to the K-Base and Reflective Notes.
- **Review: KnowledgeBase**
- **Review: Self-Reflection.**

Planner	Strategy	**Audit**	Skills Lab	Transformation	Exercise	Review

<u>**Critical Skill Areas (CSA)**</u>

<Based on your Selection Criteria Statement in Module 2 (Assignment A2-2), list here 4-5 broad Critical Skill Areas that you think are the most important for the Job (position) you described. For example, *1. Communication Skills.*>

1.

2.

3.

4.

5.

Critical Skill Subareas ("Key Competencies, or "Units of Competency")

<Broad Critical Skill Areas (such as *Communication Skills*, *Information Technology Skills*, etc.) are typically composed of several narrower subareas. For example, a broad Critical Skill Area *Communication Skills* is likely to include subareas, such as *Written Communications*, *Oral Communications*, *Presentation Skills*, etc. For each of the specified above CSAs, identify 1-3 corresponding subareas that are most relevant for the job you described in Module 2 Assignment (Those subareas are often referred to as "Key Competencies", or "Units of Competency").

#	Critical Skill Area	Corresponding Key Competencies (=Units of Competency)
1		1.1.
		1.2.
		1.3
2		2.1
		2.2
		2.3
3		3.1
		3.2.
		3.3
4		4.1
		4.2
		4.3
5		5.1
		5.2
		5.3

Elements of Competency

<Each Key Competency can be further broken apart to the level of elements so that in order to acquire the competency one will need to master all or most of the elements of that competency. For example, the key competency *Written Communication* may include several elements of competency, such as *Producing Memos*, *Preparing Executive Summaries*, *Writing Analytical Reports*, etc. For each Key Competency, specify 1-3 corresponding elements of competency that are necessary to excel on the job you described in Module 2 Assignment.>

Key Competencies ("Units")	Corresponding Elements of Competency
1.1.	1.1.1
	1.1.2
1.2.	1.2.1
	1.2.2
1.3	1.3.1
	1.3.2
2.1	2.1.1
	2.1.2
2.2	2.2.1
	2.2.2
2.3	2.3.1
	2.3.2
3.1	3.1.1

	3.1.2
3.2.	
3.3	
4.1	
4.2	
4.3	
5.1	
5.2	
5.3	

Critical Tasks. Job-Specific Skillset:

<At this point, you are supposed to have specified 4-5 broad Critical Skill Areas, 10-15 corresponding Key Competencies, and a number of related elementary competencies (can be anywhere in the range of 10-30 or even more). Now, we want you to review the resultant list of the Elements of Competency and select only 5-6 of them that you think are the most important ("critical") to succeed in the specified job. In the textbook, we call these critically important elements of competency "Critical Tasks". Once selected, a subset of critical tasks is referred to as "Job-Specific Skillset". Now, for the job you described in Module 2 please list the critical tasks:

Job Title:

Critical Tasks for the job (= Job-Specific Skillset):

1.

2.

3.

4.

5.

6.

Planner	Strategy	Audit	**Skills Lab**	Transformation	Exercise	Review

Benchmarks/Best practices:

<Please review the Job-Specific Skillset for the position you analyzed earlier. Let's switch gears again and think about how you could evaluate someone's job readiness for the position based

on the person's proficiency in performing the specified critical tasks. A typical approach utilized in performance management is to assess the person's mastery against certain standards or best practices, commonly referred to as "benchmarks". Are you aware of any standards/best practices in performing the specified above critical tasks that can be used as benchmarks? Provide some examples and, if possible, indicate where the benchmarks can be found/observed.>

#	Critical Task	Benchmark/Standard	Where to find/observe
1			
2			
3			
4			
5			
6			

Assessment Toolbox

<Methods, tools, and techniques that are used for skills assessment are based on either direct or indirect measurements of mastery (where appropriate) and/or observations (see more in the course text and recommended literature). Below, please list the methods and techniques that you think can be used for assessing the level of skills acquisition in performing each of the critical tasks in the job-specific skillset.>

#	Critical Task	Assessment methods, tools, and techniques
1		
2		
3		
4		
5		
6		

Evidence of mastery in performing the critical tasks:

<Now, we want you to switch back to a job applicant's role. Think about ways to describe and demonstrate YOUR level of proficiency in performing the above critical tasks. How would you demonstrate your proficiency and measure it against the benchmark/standard/best practice? What would you use as evidence of your mastery? Can you think of an observable artifact (primary evidence) that you can demonstrate? Or, you can provide a record (secondary evidence) showing that your mastery was already assessed (for example, by your supervisor). For each critical task in the job-specific skillset, describe your evidence (in second column) and provide a brief comment below.>

#	1. Critical Task	2. Evidence of your mastery	3. Self-assessment
1			
2			
3			
4			

5			
6			

Comments:

Self-Assessment

<An ability to conduct an accurate self-assessment of skills acquisition is an important skill in itself. In Module 4, we will discuss it in detail. Right now, we would like you to rate your perceived level of mastery against the corresponding benchmark in Column 3 above. You may use the following scale: 1 – "poor, far below the benchmark", 2- "satisfactory, still below, but approaching the benchmark", 3- "good, equal to the benchmark", 4 – "excellent, perhaps exceeding the benchmark". You will use the results of this exercise when working on the Critical Skills Assessment Tool (below). Also, you will need to describe the exercise in Assignment A3-1.>

Planner	Strategy	Audit	Skills Lab	**Transformation**	Exercise	Review

Critical Skills Assessment Tool (CSAT)

< You can think about the results of your work in the Skills Lab as a skillset review summary. This is a tangible outcome; it can be presented to your current or prospective employer. To organize the results, please download the Skills Assessment Tool (CSAT) template and follow the instructions. Submit your populated CSAT. In addition, we would like you to think more about the process of self-assessment and write a brief learning essay (Assignment 3).>

Planner	Strategy	Audit	Skills Lab	Transformation	Exercise	**Review**

Knowledgebase: My Learning Resources

<Add here 5-6 NEW resources (books, articles, websites, blogs etc.) that are useful for your ongoing professional development. Please do not include either the course textbook, or resources cited in the textbook.>

1.

2.

3.

4.

5.

Reflective Notes

<Explain in 2-3 paragraphs the main topics and ideas discussed in this Module. What have you learned? Do not cite the textbook here, use your own words.>

Notes:

Review "My Career Summary Statement", "Professional Skills", "Generic Skills", "Career Self-Management Skills"

<Do you think that based on your self-assessment you will need to review/revise some of your Summary and Skills documents in Modules 1-2? Revise if needed and explain below in 1-2 paragraphs.>

CPW-3 SUBMISSION:

When finished, submit the Career Self-Management E-Portfolio & Workbook in the designated box. Please do not cut and paste; just keep working in the Workbook continuously and every time submit the entire Workbook file. Due date: see Course Schedule.

Module 4: Managing Your Skills Lab

Planner	Strategy	Audit	Skills Lab	Transformation	Exercise	Review

Module 4 Tasks:

1. **Example: CSD.** You should begin this module by downloading and reviewing a populated sample of the Critical Skill Dashboard (CSD) Tool.
2. **Readings R4/Videos C4.** Then, read the text, content guides, and assigned articles.
3. **Discussion D4.** In the discussion, we want you to focus on the concept of Quantified Self.
4. **CPW4.** After that we want you to move to the Skills Lab section in the Workbook and work on developing a personalized version of the CSD Tool.
   - **Skills Lab**
   - **Transformation**
   - **Audit**
5. **Assignments A4.** These exercises are designed to report the results of your skillset review.
6. **CPW4.** To complete the Module, please add to the K-Base and Reflective Notes.
   - **Review: KnowledgeBase**
   - **Review: Self-Reflection.**

Planner	Strategy	Audit	**Skills Lab**	Transformation	Exercise	Review

A sample Critical Skill Dashboard (CSD) Tool

<To begin, please download the Critical Skill Dashboard EXAMPLE (pdf), review it, and read the instructions.>

The Total Skillset Score (T.S.S.)

<When considering applicants for a job, employers often norm selection criteria by assigning numerical weights. Let us see how it is done in the provided CSD. Please note that the total of weights is 100 meaning that an ideal candidate for the job will score 100 points. Now, we can calculate the T.S.S. (or the Total Skillset Score) for any candidate if we know their subscores (performance levels). If, for example, the weight of Written Communications is 20% and the candidate's performance level is 2 (out of 4), then the subscore for Written Communications is 10 (out of 20). In the example provided the T.T.S. of the prospective candidate is 66.5 which clearly indicates that there is plenty of room for growth. If you were the candidate, how would you calculate your T.S.S.?>

Comments:

Your (self-assessed) Critical Skill Dashboard

<Now, it is time to practice! Download the Critical Skill Dashboard Template, fill it in with your data using the above example and the information you collected for Skills Assessment Tool (CSAT) in Module 3.>

The accuracy of assessment

<In Module 3, you used self-assessment to evaluate your mastery in performing the critical tasks. But how accurate was your self-assessment? Can you get the same piece of evidence evaluated by an expert or one of your peers? Ideally, you should be able to use all three methods.

#	Critical Task	Self-assessment	Peer-assessment	Expert assessment
1				
2				
3				
4				
5				
6				

Feedback seeking and preserving evidence:

<Provide here your plan for collecting evidence and getting it evaluated by experts and peers. How would you record their evaluations? Where would you store them? Where and how would you use them?>

Comments:

My T.S.S.

< Now, you are in a position to calculate your Total Skillset Score for the position you specified in Module 2 Assignment and estimate your likely standing in the job competition in relation to the ideal candidate. The more honest you are in your self-assessment, the more accurate your T.S.S. is going to be. So, what is your T.S.S.? What does it tell you? Please explain in Assignment 4.>

My critical skill advantages, parities, and gaps

<You can also visualize your findings in relation to your competitive standing for the position you specified in Module 2 assignment. You can see where your skills are on par with an ideal candidate (let's call it your competitive advantage and use green color) and where you are close enough to the requirements (your competitive parities can be labelled yellow). Also, where there are gaps in your preparation (red color). Some gaps may be minor and some severe. We will ask you to reflect on this exercise in Assignment 4.>

Planner	Strategy	Audit	Skills Lab	**Transformation**	Exercise	Review

My Critical Skills Dashboard (CSD) and Total Skillset Score (TSS)

<Complete your self-assessed CSD and submit it in the A4 submission box. Please note that this result is a tangible outcome of the course and can be used in your job application (promotion) interview. In addition, the Assignment requires you to provide comments for your CSD and TSS.>

Planner	Strategy	**Audit**	Skills Lab	Transformation	Exercise	Review

Review "My personal, skill-based SWOT Analysis" (Module 2)

<We think that based on the results of your self-assessment in Modules 3 and 4 you may need to review/revise some of your personal SWOT Analysis results in Module 2. Revise if needed and explain below in 1-2 paragraphs.>

SWOT Analysis revisions:

Planner	Strategy	Audit	Skills Lab	Transformation	Exercise	Review

Knowledgebase: My Learning Resources

<Add here 5-6 NEW resources (books, articles, websites, blogs etc.) that are useful for your ongoing professional development. Please do not include either the course textbook, or resources cited in the textbook.>

1.
2.
3.
4.
5.
6.

Reflective Notes

<Explain in 2-3 paragraphs the main topics and ideas discussed in this Module. What have you learned? Do not cite the textbook here, use your own words.>

My Notes:

Review "My Career Summary Statement", "Professional Skills", "Generic Skills", "Career Self-Management Skills"

<Do you think that based on your self-assessment you will need to review/revise some of your Summary and Skills documents in Modules 1-3? Revise if needed and explain below in 1-2 paragraphs.>

CPW-4 SUBMISSION:

When finished, submit the Career Self-Management E-Portfolio & Workbook in the designated box. Please do not cut and paste; just keep working in the Workbook continuously and every time submit the entire Workbook file. Due date: see Course Schedule.

Module 5: Transformation: Self-Marketing and Personal Branding

Planner	Strategy	Audit	Skills Lab	Transformation	Exercise	Review

Module 5 Tasks:

1. **Readings R5/Videos C5.** Start by reading the text, content guides, and assigned articles.
2. **CPW5.** Then, you should move to the Strategy and Audit in the Workbook.
   - **Strategy**
   - **Audit.**
3. **Discussion D5.** After that reflect on your self-marketing skills in the discussion.
4. **CPW5.** Then, you should move to the Skills Lab section in the Workbook.
   - **Skills Lab**
   - **Transformation and Exercise.**
5. **Assignments A5.** These exercises will help reporting your transformative experiences.
6. **CPW5.** In the end, add to the K-Base and Reflective Notes.
   - **Strategy: SMPBP (Self-Marketing and Personal Branding Plan)**
   - **Review: KnowledgeBase**
   - **Review: Self-Reflection.**

Planner	Strategy	Audit	Skills Lab	Transformation	Exercise	Review

My Personal (Career) Brand

<People tend to think about human brands as something only related to celebrities. Meanwhile, the concept of branding is highly relevant in the career development context. By definition, "brand" is an image of the product in the consumer's mind. Likewise, you may think of your career brand as an image of your professional self in the prospective employer's mind. Now, please review your Career Summary Statement in Module 1. What do you think a prospective employer is likely to conclude about your skills based on that document? What is that you want them to think? Is it well communicated? Do you need to strengthen your message?

Enter comments here (you may also want to revise your Career Summary Statement in Module 1).

Planner	Strategy	**Audit**	Skills Lab	Transformation	Exercise	Review

A Skilled (Professional) Self

<As shown in the text, it is helpful to think about your skills as a value proposition. It is like if you were a highly skilled professional offering your services to prospective clients. (Think about lawyers, doctors, financial planners, etc.) The problem with promoting services is that they are intangible and inseparable from their consumption. So, to convince someone to buy a service, the service salesman must utilize a range of special techniques commonly referred to as "professional services marketing". Keeping in mind that the product (service) here is your skillset, how would you describe yourself as a skilled professional? Please explain.>

Comments:

Utilizing your CSD: a data-driven, evidence-based, and externally verified tool

<When working on the above task, you may have found that to make your value proposition stronger, it would have been better to rely on a data-driven, evidence-based, and externally verified approach. For this purpose, you may utilize the CSD tool that you developed in Module 4 for the position specified in Module 2. To begin, review the green areas in your CSD that demonstrate your proven strengths in performing the critical tasks. If you did all the required work in Module 4, then you have already obtained, verified, and quantified the evidence of your mastery. How would you incorporate this information into a concise and energetic statement summarizing your mastery of skills (your USP)?>

Your USP (=Unique Selling Proposition)

< What is your USP (unique selling proposition) for a prospective employer based on their needs and your strengths (demonstrated competencies)? Please explain. You may have already noted that your USP is not universal; in other words, you will need to tweak it for every new position based on the job requirements and your skillset review.>

Position (job) and job requirements:

My USP:

Your self-marketing skills

<How good do you think you are at demonstrating and promoting your skills? Please explain here.>

My self-marketing skills:

Planner	Strategy	Audit	Skills Lab	Transformation	Exercise	Review

Self-marketing as a career competency (skill) (The 7P Framework)

<You can improve your self-marketing skills, if you think about them as an important career competency. To approach self-marketing more professionally, you can learn from the discipline of marketing. Of particular interest is the field known as "professional services marketing". The foundational model of services marketing is called 7P, as it describes the seven, most important components of services marketing (product, price, place, promotion, people, processes, and physical evidence). Now, if you used the same 7P framework for self-marketing of your skills when applying for the position you specified in Module 2, what would be the most important factors for you to consider? To answer this question, we recommend that you populate the table below. Once again, please note that this is not a one-size-fits-all approach. In other words, for each position the 7P table needs to be slightly (or significantly) modified.

	7 P components	Description	How to use: strategies and tools
1	Product/service	<You are your skills. Define here your skillset for the job>	Current credentials, experiences, functional resume, bio sketch
2	Price/value	You are selling not yourself but your skills as a solution to the employer's problems.	Your USP – think about how to incorporate it in your cover letter and during your job interview

3	Place/Positioning	Your skills need to closely match the job requirements.	Selection criteria statement, covering letter, certifications
4	Promotional mix and packaging	This is how you showcase and demonstrate your skills.	LinkedIn, recorded presentations, professional publications.
5	People	There must be other people to support your claims.	Networking, social media, job references, peer reviews
6	Physical evidence	Hard evidence + argument = the best proof of your skills	Selection criteria statement, work samples, other evidence
7	Process/Productivity	You need to be a team player, with a growth mindset.	Think how to show personal skills and a positive attitude.

Self-marketing KSA (knowledge, skills, and attitudes)

As a complex competency, self-marketing has three dimensions: cognitive (knowledge), behavioral (skills), and affective (attitude). Oftentimes, the behavioral dimension receives the most attention ("self-marketing as a skill in itself"), while the underpinning knowledge (for example, the 7P model of services marketing) is used on the need-to-know basis. The affective dimension is often left behind, because many people are shy or just do not like the very idea of self-marketing or personal branding. A negative attitude to self-marketing may hinder professional growth so that it needs to be addressed. A practical approach is to use exercises like "The Elevator Pitch" in a safe and trusted environment to build confidence, develop necessary habits, and become accustomed to, well, some bragging about yourself.

Provide here your thoughts about your attitude to self-marketing and personal branding. Why and where do you think you may need it? Do you feel comfortable doing it? How do you think other people come to terms with themselves and engage in self-promotion in a positive way?

Comments:

Self-marketing as a skill

By now, you should be able to analyze any competency by breaking it down into corresponding units and elements (critical tasks). Using the same approach, you can think about your self-marketing skills as a CSA (Critical Skill Area). Then, you can break it down to 4-5 key competencies. Please note that there is no "right" way of doing this. How to define key competencies and critical tasks will depend on your particular situation and typical approaches that are used by successful professionals, recruiters, and employers in your field. Also, you should think about other relevant skills (like digital fluency and social media marketing) that you can showcase when presenting your skillset to a potential employer. Here are some of the examples of key competencies, with related elements of competency (critical tasks).

	CSA	Key competencies (units)	Critical tasks
1	Skills Analysis	. Analyze the job.	Identify the required skillset
		. Analyze your readiness	Conduct an accurate skillset review
2	Job Application	2.1. Use resume to present skills	Skill-based (functional) resume
		2.2. Create USP to stand out	Incorporate USP in the cover letter
		2.3. Respond to selection criteria	Use Selection Criteria Statement
3	Public Profile	3.1. Advertise your skills	Use LinkedIn profile
		3.2. Showcase work samples	Use LinkedIn portfolio feature
4	Communication Skills	4.1. Interviewing skills	Use impression management
		4.2. Persuasion	Use elevator pitch
5	Search for Opportunities	5.1. Resourcefulness	Use Networking, Events
		5.2. Digital self-marketing	Use Social Media, blogging

Using benchmarks and assessment tools for honing self-marketing skills

<After you have identified the critical tasks, you should be looking for appropriate benchmarks, best practices, and role models. For example, what would be an exemplary way to use a LinkedIn profile in your case? Do you know how to use it properly? Is there any checklist (=a self-assessment tool) that could tell you that your LinkedIn profile indeed does the job you want it to do? Or, may be, there is a way to obtain a peer or even expert evaluation of your LinkedIn profile. But how would you arrange it?>

Comments:

Organizing your stuff: The ABC portfolio

<Finding suitable benchmarks, standards or best practices may present a challenge. So, when you find a good example or a resource, it does make sense to store it somewhere on the cloud in a sort of e-portfolio for benchmarks (we will call it a "b-portfolio"). Yet another section of that electronic portfolio can be used for storing assessment tools and resources ("a-portfolio"). Finally, your own work samples that you collect for training and development purposes and can use as evidence of your mastery in performing critical skills can be stored in your career portfolio (or a "c-portfolio"). But where would you keep those portfolios?>

Comments:

My public (professional) profile

<What you do in your Skills Lab is your private business and you probably do not need to share it with anyone except a mentor, career coach, or a trusted peer reviewer. But how do you tell the world that you have transformed into a skilled professional? For this purpose, you will need to create a public (professional) profile. Your public profile is a carefully selected collection of artifacts that is supposed to best represent your professional self for external audiences. An old-age, traditional way to create a public profile is to use a resume, a CV, a bio sketch, a professional publication, a newspaper article about you, or a reference letter. In the digital era, a public profile is created with the use of LinkedIn, social media, websites and blogging, and other means that can be used to communicate and showcase your skills. So, what is your public profile and what do you want it to be?

Comments:

Self-marketing communications mix

<Your career brand is your professional image in the eyes of your colleagues and potential employers. As you can learn from the discipline of marketing, brands can be successfully managed. Creating an informative and powerful public profile is a very important step for managing your career brand. Also, it is not a one-time activity, as your skills portfolio and the level of expertise will be growing over time. In terms of the most relevant marketing approach for building an effective public profile, you can build on the concept of service marketing communications mix (see the 7P Framework in the text and assigned readings).

Marketing communications mix includes several components and activities that help potential customers learn about the brand and its unique characteristics, relate them to their needs, and eventually come to a buying decision. The components and activities include advertising, direct marketing, personal selling, sales promotion, and PR. The same approach can be used for self-marketing, where a public profile takes the place of advertising. The goals of advertising are to not just make a potential buyer aware of the brand but to also create interest and desire to act. Do you think your public profile should serve the same goals? If yes, how this can be achieved?>

Comments:

My LinkedIn account

<LinkedIn (www.linkedin.com) is one of the most popular tools for creating a professional public profile. It combines a resume, a career portfolio (with work samples), and a platform for peer reviewing and networking. Also, the LinkedIn Resume Assistant plugin, which is a new addition to MS Word, is very helpful in identifying key competencies and critical tasks.

In this course we assume that you have already created a LinkedIn profile. Does it serve its goal and what the goal is? What is the advertising message that your LinkedIn profile is supposed to carry? How do you think other people do it? Are you aware of any exemplary LinkedIn profiles in your professional field? What makes them exemplary? Can you think of an assessment rubric for a LinkedIn portfolio? Can you create a rubric to use for your LinkedIn profile? How would you rate yourself? How do you think you can improve?

Comments:

Career portfolio

<As mentioned earlier, a career portfolio ("c-portfolio") is a collection of your work samples to be presented to potential employers for demonstrating your mastery of skills. It can be actual samples or observations of your work made by experts, supervisors, and peers. Also, it can be a collection of certifications and badges. Having samples is helpful for demonstrating your mastery but you may not be allowed to showcase the actual work you have done for other employers. One way of demonstrating your skills is to use a self-talk in the form of a slide or video presentation. You may find it useful to store it in a publicly available platform (like, "YouTube" or "SlideShare") and reference on your LinkedIn account.>

Did you see other people's presentations linked to their LinkedIn accounts? How did they di it? Was it done well? What did it tell you about their skills? Would you be willing to use the same approach? Yes or no – and why? Please explain.

Comments:

My active behaviors

<One can only achieve positive career outcomes through active behaviors, such as job market scanning, new job applications, promotion requests, skill building, career skills development, and personal skills development for career growth and self-realization. In a limited time that working adults have for their continuing education and professional development, they often neglect investing into developing their career building skills – probably because those skills are typically not explicitly mentioned in job advertisements. In this course we advocate for taking career development skills more seriously; for example, by paying attention to self-marketing skills. In this Module, we will explore how you can use a powerful self-marketing communication tool known as "Elevator Pitch" to promote your USP for the position you specified in Module 2.

What is an Elevator Pitch?

<In the assignment 5, we will ask you to conduct a thorough research on elevator pitch as a marketing communication strategy. You will also need to analyze it as a skill, find out benchmarks and assessment tools, and come up with a message map for your USP, peer-assessment strategy, and a self-assessment tool. Then, you will need to flex your digital muscles, create and record a powerful pitch, and get it peer reviewed.>

Comments:

Your Elevator Pitch as a self-administered training intervention

<It may happen that you are already a highly qualified elevator pitcher, but most students are usually not. Even more, many people do not feel comfortable with either speaking publicly, or recording and showcasing themselves, or speaking about own skills. But in a skill-based, competitive job environment, having this skill is a must. So, what we will do is to arrange a self-administered training intervention in a safe and trusted environment. As you are now familiar with your small group and you are not in a competitive situation, we invite you to work collectively on this, not very easy task, and help yourself and each other. In the end, you should be able to produce a well-written, persuasive, energetic, and well-recorded pitch introducing your USP for the position in Module 2. We also expect that you will peer review two-three other people presentations and provide a friendly, but honest and helpful developmental feedback. The intended outcome of this activity is that you will be able to better: 1) analyze your skillset; 2) connect it to your personal strengths and abilities; 3) relate to the prospective employer's interest; 4) express it succinctly and persuasively.

Comments:

Planner	Strategy	Audit	Skills Lab	Transformation	Exercise	Review

My Self-Marketing and Personal Branding Plan (Showcaser): How to's

<Your Self-Marketing and Personal Branding Plan (SMPBP) is to help you organize, guide, and evaluate your active self-marketing behaviors aimed at reaching your strategic career development goals. One way of doing it is to promote and showcase your strengths identified as green areas in your CSPD (Critical Skills Profiler and Dashboard) in Module 4. To begin, review the green areas in your CSPD that demonstrate your proven strengths in performing the critical tasks. Then, you should describe precisely what contributed to the high level of your mastery in performing these tasks. Please review the following (fictitious) example where we suppose that the three critical tasks highlighted green are as follows:

	Critical Task	**Description of competitive advantage: I scored highly in**
1.2.1	Analytical reports	- Theoretical analysis (assumptions, models, narrative); - Discussion (what problem you have solved).
2.2.1.	PPT presentations	- Effectively presenting to large groups; - The use of visual aids and animations.
3.1.1.	Advanced MS Excel skills	- Using VBA variables and writing macros; - Power Pivot tables and pivot reporting.

If the above were your results, they would represent your competitive advantage in a data-driven, evidence-based, and externally verified way. But how to communicate these findings to a prospective employer? To do so, you will need to create a promotional strategy for each of your skills (green areas). It may look as follows:

	Critical Task	Action items for self-promotion	Timeline
1.2.1	Analytical reports	Identify an exemplary report for showcasing; Arrange expert evaluation with praise of its key elements; Place it in your c-portfolio on the cloud; Link to your LinkedIn profile.	
2.2.1.	PPT presentations	Identify an exemplary PPT presentation; Place in SlideShare, arrange expert evaluation; Link to your LinkedIn profile.	
3.1.1.	Advanced MS Excel skills	Identify an example demonstrating your mastery of using VBA and pivot tables; Think creatively about how to present it (may be, using a short video); Link to your LinkedIn account.	

My Self-Marketing and Personal Branding Plan (=Showcaser)

<Download the template, complete your SMPB Plan and submit it in the Assignment A5-1 area. Elevator Pitch is the second part of this assignment.>

Planner	Strategy	Audit	Skills Lab	Transformation	Exercise	Review

My Functional Resume or LinkedIn (optional)

<Functional resume is one where you highlight your mastery of skills. You may google it to find examples. You may have used this approach already; in this case, just review it and see whether you need to make some adjustments based on your self-analysis. Work on your functional resume and submit it as an attachment to the Workbook file. You may also notice that LinkedIn uses a similar (functional) approach highlighting mastery of skills. >

Comments:

Planner	Strategy	Audit	Skills Lab	Transformation	Exercise	Review

Knowledgebase: My Learning Resources

<Add here 5-6 resources (books, articles, websites, blogs etc.) that are useful for your ongoing professional development. Please do not include either the course textbook, or resources cited in the textbook.>

1.
2.
3.
4.
5.
6.

Reflective Notes

<Explain in 2-3 paragraphs the main topics and ideas discussed in this Module. What have you learned? Do not cite the textbook here, use your own words.>

Notes:

Review "My Career Summary Statement", "Professional Skills", "Generic Skills", "Career Self-Management Skills"

<Do you think that based on your self-assessment you will need to review/revise some of your Summary and Skills documents in Modules 1-3? Revise if needed and explain below in 1-2 paragraphs.>

CPW-5 SUBMISSION:

When finished, submit the Career Self-Management E-Portfolio & Workbook in the designated box. Please do not cut and paste; just keep working in the Workbook continuously and every time submit the entire Workbook file. Attach your functional resume as a separate file. Due date: see Course Schedule.

Module 6: Effective Regulation for SMARTER Outcomes

Planner	Strategy	Audit	Skills Lab	Transformation	Exercise	Review

Module 6 Tasks:

1. **Readings R6/Videos C6.** Start by reading the text, content guides, and assigned articles.
2. **CPW6.** Then, you should move to the Exercise section in the Workbook.
   - **Exercise**
3. **Discussion D6.** In the discussion, review three elevator pitch submissions by your peers and provide an evaluation using an appropriate rubric.
4. **CPW6.** Then, you should move to the Skills Lab section in the Workbook.
   - **Skills Lab**
   - **Audit**
5. **Assignments A6.** This exercise is to work on your Skill-Building Plan.
6. **CPW6.** To complete the Module, work in the Review and Strategy sections.
   - **Review: KnowledgeBase**
   - **Review: Self-Reflection.**
   - **Strategy**
7. **After you have finished Module 6 tasks, review and submit the entire Workbook.**

Planner	Strategy	Audit	Skills Lab	Transformation	Exercise	Review

My active behaviors

<As described in Module 5, one can only achieve positive career outcomes through active behaviors, such as job market scanning, new job applications, promotion requests, skill building, career skills development, and personal skills development for career growth and self-realization. Given a limited time that working adults have for continuing education and professional development, how would you know that you are using your time effectively and efficiently? In this Module, we'll explore some important components of active behaviors, such as feedback seeking and goal setting behaviors.>

Comments:

Feedback seeking behavior: Conducting a thorough peer-review

<When considering your skill building ability in previous modules as a skill in its own right, you have learned that receiving an accurate and just-in-time assessment of your skills is crucially important. It should not come as a surprise that career researchers consider feedback seeking behavior as a precursor of successful career building. But how can one arrange and organize this activity? As an exercise, in this Module you will receive feedback on your Elevator Pitch by your fellow classmates. Also, you will also observe their work and provide feedback. What are your thoughts about their peer-assessment of your work? Were you able to communicate your USP? Why?

Comments:

Goal setting behavior and SMARTER goals

<Goal setting behavior is another well-know characteristic feature of successful career builders. You have probably heard already about the usefulness of so-called SMARTER goals where "SMARTER" stands for Specific, Measurable, Achievable, Realistic, and Time-Bound goals. The idea behind SMARTER goals is that you would be much better positioned for success if you knew for sure what to achieve, how to do it, and how to measure the progress provided that the goal is indeed exactly what you need, and it is within a reach. However, the problem with SMARTER goals is that it is not that easy to define them correctly and to find a way to measure success. That's why it is a big advantage to have a mentor or an experienced career coach who could do it for you. You can also learn how to effectively self-coach and establish SMARTER goals for your particular situation by yourself. To find out, we'll continue this Module in the Skills Lab.>

Comments:

Active regulation

<The theory behind establishing work-related SMARTER goals is called active regulation (see more in the Readings). The idea of active regulation is to thoroughly review your workplace situation and the required skillset, then evaluate your existing skillset against the relevant benchmark, identify strengths, parities, and weaknesses, and after that design and execute a very concrete and detailed plan for improvement. The very fortunate thing is that in Modules 3-4 you have already learned most of it. Now, you need to go back to the CSD tool to find out how it can used for establishing and monitoring your SMARTER goals.>

Comments:

Using your CSD (Critical Skills Dashboard) for self-improvement

<In your CSD (Module 4) review the area labelled yellow and red where some significant (or major) improvements are required in order you can get a higher T.S.S. (total skillset score). This is how it may look like:

	Critical Task	Description of problems: I scored low in (.) because of (.)
1.2.1	Analytical reports	- Weak theoretical analysis (assumptions, models, narrative);
3.1.1.	Advanced MS Excel skills	- Do not use VBA variables and writing macros; - Cannot work with Pivot tables.

The important thing is to specify in detail what the problem is, what is your current level and what a desired level would be (for example, you may find out that if you were at least an intermediate level specialist in Advanced MS Excel, then your overall T.S.S, for the position would be, say, 75% instead of current 58%). This information should be enough to provide you with S.M.A.R.T.E.R. goals for your Skill-Building Plan.>

Comments:

"My Skill Building Plan (SBP)"

< Download and complete the Skill Building Plan Template and submit it in A6 submission area.>

My skill-building activity as a self-administered training intervention

<When you decide to engage in self-initiated, skill building activities, it is helpful to think about it as a self-administered training intervention where you play the roles of both the athlete and the coach. As an athlete, you keep tirelessly training. As a coach, you are responsible for setting goals and monitoring the progress. Also, you should be thinking about how to instill confidence, provide support and give constructive feedback, and provide training evaluation in the end. Is it at all possible? How do other people do it? Is there any theory behind it that I can use? This is where you may probably want to take a course in positive psychology and test your SDL skills.>

Comments:

Planner	Strategy	Audit	Skills Lab	Transformation	Exercise	Review

"My self-directed learning (SDL) skills"

<To become your own career development coach, you will need to learn how to effectively guide and direct your own learning. In Module 2 readings and content guides we introduced two concepts that are the most useful for this purpose, self-directed learning (SDL) and self-regulated learning (SRL). Also, we recommended that you read very informative and powerful articles on the subject by J. Mezirow and E. Zimmerman. Now it's time to reflect and self-assess your SDL skills here.>

Comments:

How confident are you in your ability to excel in skill building and sustain the career self-management effort?

Do you remember a story about a little engine that could? Believing in own capabilities does matter, as proven by many researchers. In the end, we would like you to get familiar with some works of Alex Bandura on self-efficacy and think about how it is relevant for your endurance and career success. You will also have a chance to reflect on your readings in the Review section and while working on Assignment 6.

Planner	Strategy	Audit	Skills Lab	Transformation	Exercise	Review

Knowledgebase: My Learning Resources

<Add here 5-6 NEW resources (books, articles, websites, blogs etc.) that are useful for your ongoing professional development. Please do not include either the course textbook, or resources cited in the textbook.>

1.
2.
3.
4.
5.
6.

Reflective Notes

<Explain in 2-3 paragraphs the main topics and ideas discussed in this Module. What have you learned? Do not cite the textbook here, use your own words.>

Notes:

Self-Audit: The most important thing that you have learned in the course

<Overall, what have you learned in this course? Can you think of one, the most important takeaway?>

CPW-6 AND the FINAL SUBMISSION:

When finished, submit the Career Self-Management E-Portfolio & Workbook in the designated box. Please do not cut and paste; just keep working in the Workbook continuously and every time submit the entire Workbook file. Due date: see Course Schedule.

Module 7: Reflection and Reinforcement: Career Self-Management Workflow

Planner						
	Strategy	Audit	Skills Lab	Transformation	Exercise	Review

Module 7 Tasks:

1. **Readings R7/Videos C7.** Start by reading the text and content guides.
2. **Review:** Complete and submit Post-test self-audit (Assignment 7)
3. **Strategy:** Think about your ongoing Career Self-Management strategy (see below)
4. **Skills Lab:** Review introductory video for "*How to Get Skilled*" on "Coursera"
5. **Exercise:** Review suggested OneNote CSM Workbook.

	Strategy					
Planner		Audit	Skills Lab	Transformation	Exercise	Review

Your Career Self-Management strategy and tactics

<In the end of the course it is a good idea to think about your career self-management strategy in general and some tactical ways of implementing it. For example, how would you answer the following questions:

6. Have you decided about your career growth scenarios?
7. Did you schedule your active behaviors?
8. Do you have a skill-building plan?
9. Do you have a self-marketing & personal branding plan?
10. How are you going to organize your career self-management workflow?

Your next step: How to organize an effective Career Self-Management Workflow

Module 7 is a bonus part of the course where we share some ideas about how to incorporate career self-management in your daily routines. For example, you may want to explore a new tool, OneNote CSM Workbook. You can download it in the course. You will see that this is the same Workbook that you are using in the course. But it is done in a free Microsoft software called OneNote. OneNote is actually an electronic journal and a diary. You can use it as an ABC portfolio as discussed earlier. You can use it as a career fitness diary following the logic we presented in this course. It is all in one place, accessible on your phone/tablet and integrated with other Microsoft software.

Yet another thing you may be interested in is to take an advanced version of this course on Coursera. It is only one week long but there are more tools and practical applications. See you in the course!

Appendix 1

Assignment A1: Pre-Test Self-Audit

Student:		ID	
Area of Studies:		Concentration	
Term, year:		Instructor	

Task 1: Answer questions 1-10 by assigning levels of importance. Please provide a brief rationale.
A) Little important; B) somewhat important; C) quite important; D) critically important.

#	Question	A	B	C	D	Rationale
	How important do you think each of the following is to the employment success of new graduates of the degree program in your chosen field (concentration)?	A	B	C	D	
1	Writing clearly and effectively					
2	Speaking clearly and persuasively					
3	Thinking analytically					
4	Analyzing quantitative problems					
5	Using information technology effectively					
6	Working effectively with others					
7	Understanding people of other racial and ethnic backgrounds					
8	Developing a personal code of values and ethics					
9	Learning effectively on your own					
10	Having well-developed career building skills (job market analysis, self-assessment, skill building, self-management)					

Note: Please answer honestly. The grade for this assignment will be solely based on the timeliness and fullness of your response (do not skip questions!)

Career Building Skills Pre-Test

Task 2: Answer questions 11-22 by indicating your level of agreement on the following statements and provide a brief rationale.
Levels of agreement: 1 – "Strongly Disagree", 2 – "Disagree", 3- "Not sure", 4- "Agree", 5- "Strongly Agree".

#	Question	Response ("X")						Brief Comment (Rationale for your answer)
		n/a	1	2	3	4	5	
	I am fully confident in my ability to:							
11	Use a job search engine or similar tools to identify a prospective job matching my skills and interests							
12	Analyze job requirements and clarify the knowledge, skills, and abilities that are required on the job							
13	Identify specific critical skills/tasks/experiences that I need to master/demonstrate to best qualify for the desired job							
14	Identify benchmarks (standards, best practices) that represent the expert level of skill acquisition for my desired job							
15	Using peer- and self-assessment, objectively evaluate my current level of skill acquisition against the specified benchmarks and the likely competition							
16	Based on the assessment results, identify my strengths and competency gaps and clarify professional development needs for mastering the specified critical skills/tasks for my desired job							
17	Set specific, quantifiable targets (S.M.A.R.T. goals) for guiding skill-building activities that will enable me to master the critical skills/tasks at the required level so that I can stand out in the job selection process							

Note: Please answer honestly. The grade for this assignment will be solely based on the timeliness and fullness of your response (do not skip questions!)

18	Effectively organize and manage my skill-building activities to reach the required level of skills acquisition							
19	Create an effective functional resume emphasizing my mastery of skills required on the job							
20	Plan and undertake effective self-marketing activities to demonstrate and promote my strengths in skill acquisition at the required level							
21	Effectively utilize social media for self-promotion							
22	Overall, effectively organize my career planning, development and growth (change)							

Note: Please answer honestly. The grade for this assignment will be solely based on the timeliness and fullness of your response (do not skip questions!)

Appendix 2

Assignment A2: Position Description and Key Selection Criteria Statement

Assignment A2: Position Description and Key Selection Criteria Statement

Your Name __________ ______________ **Term, year** ______________

Organization

<Add a paragraph here briefly describing the organization (either real or fictitious) that you would like to use as an example of a prospective employer in this assignment.>

Job (Position) Title and Summary

<Add a paragraph here describing a job/position (better to cite a real job but it can also be made-up) that you would like to get with the above organization in near future. Think about a position where the successful applicant is required to have a college degree and a range of job-specific skills.>

Key Responsibilities

<Specify 5-8 key job duties/responsibilities that can best describe the above position.>

1.

2.

3.

4.

5.

6.

7.

8.

The Sample Key Selection Criteria (REVIEW ONLY)

<Selection Criteria are intended to best describe the required skills/attributes of the successful candidate. The employer's duty is to prepare a list of Key Selection Criteria to help selecting the best possible candidate for the job. The list below is a guide only; please review it and think about how to modify it for the above position.>

1. **Communication skills:** Demonstrated excellent written and oral communication skills, with the ability to prepare business memos, analytical reports, executive summaries and conduct oral presentations.
2. **Information management:** Experience/understanding of information technology and systems appropriate to the chosen field.
3. **Analytical and problem-solving skills:** Well developed analytical, problem solving skills and a demonstrated understanding of quantitative tools appropriate to the chosen field.
4. **Understanding people in an organizational context:** Demonstrated skills in developing and managing relationships with a diverse range of stakeholders and cross-functional teams.
5. **Understanding organizations within broader contexts:** An ability to effectively function in a complex and changing world and adapt to diversity, political, international, technological or environmental issues.
6. **Personal, interpersonal skills and attitudes**: A demonstrated ability to lead and manage a team in an area of high volume and high intensity workload; excellent planning, organizing and time management skills, with the ability to balance competing work priorities.

The Key Selection Criteria

<Now, it is time for you to identify the Selection Criteria for the above position. You may want to use some of the above-mentioned criteria; also, you may want to modify them and/or add other criteria as you see appropriate for the position. If you are not sure, please ask other students or contact the instructor.>

#	The Criterion	Description (what competency a successful applicant must have or be proficient at)
1		
2		
3		
4		
5		
6		

INSTRUCTIONS for A2-1:

1. *When working on Assignment A2-1 Job Description, you will act as an employer. First, use this template to specify Organization, Job Title, and Key Responsibilities.*
2. *Then, you should review the sample list of Key Selection Criteria and think about how to modify it for the job. Think about the most important skills for the job and how you would know that a certain applicant is the best one. For example, if you think that IT (information technology) skills are critically important for the job, what exactly should you use as a selection criterion? Could it be proficiency in MS Excel at a certain level? When deciding on a criterion, you should think about those that are demonstratable and assessible.*
3. *Then, populate the above table with the Key Selection Criteria for the job you have specified and submit the populated template in the designated box.*

INSTRUCTIONS for A2-2:

4. *When working on Assignment A2-2 Selection Criteria Statement, you will act as a prospective employee. Your task is to write a detailed response to the Key Selection Criteria that you specified in A2-1. Your response is a 2-4-page essay that may be written in the form of an extended covering letter. Most importantly, your essay must include a detailed response to each of the Selection Criteria explaining how YOU meet the criteria (this is the central part of your assignment). Your response should indicate that you are familiar with the requirement and you have demonstratable evidence of your mastery of the required skill.*
5. *Please do not skip any criterion. If you think that a certain criterion is relevant, but you haven't mastered it yet, explain what your current level is and how you can improve it.*
6. *Please format and proofread your paper as appropriate. The expected length of the paper is 2-4 pages (Arial or Times Roman, font size 12, single or double spaced).*
7. *When finished, submit your paper in the designated box. Please only use .docx, or .rtf formats (other formats, such as pdf, open office, etc., are not acceptable).*

Appendix 3

Assignment A3: Critical Skills Assessment Tool (CSAT) Template

Critical Skills Assessment Tool (CSAT) Template. Version 2020

Student Name: ______________________ ____________________________ Term, Year: __________________________

1	2	3	4	5	6	7
Critical Skill Areas (CSA)	**CSA Subareas (Key Competencies or Units)**	**Critical Tasks (Competency elements)**	**Benchmark (Standard)**	**Evidence of your mastery on file**	**Assessment method/technique**	**Self-Assessment results (rating)**
Example: **Communication skills**	*Examples:* Written communications Oral communications	*Examples:* - Writing a memo; - Preparing an executive summary; - Conducting a virtual presentation.	*Example:* - Company guidelines; - Certification; - Best Practice; - Role Model; - Industry standard	*Example:* - Sample memo; - Sample report; - Recorded presentation; - Industry award; - Reference.	*Example:* - Method: expert, peer, self-assessment; - Technique: Observation, checklist; rubric.	- 1 -poor - 2 - satisfactory; - 3 - good; - 4 –excellent (equivalent to or exceeding the benchmark).
1. <add>	1.1<add>	1.1.1<add>	<add>	<add>	<add>	<add>
		1.1.2				
	1.2<add>					
2.<add>	2.1<add>					
	2.2<add>					
3.<add>	3.1<add>					
	3.2<add>					
4.<add>	4.1<add>					
	4.2<add>					
5.<add>	5.1<add>					
	5.2<add>					

INSTRUCTIONS:

1. *This template is provided to help you working on your CSAT (Critical Skills Assessment Tool) in the Module 3 section of the Workbook.*
2. *First, you work on the tasks 12-17 in the Workbook. Then, you can populate the template as instructed below.*
3. *In Column 1, enter 4-5 Critical Skill Areas (CSA). For example, "1. Communication Skills".*
4. *In Column 2, for each CSA enter 1-2 corresponding CSA Subareas (= Key Competencies, also known as "Units of Competency"). For example, for CSA "1. Communications Skills" you may enter "1.1. Written Communications", "1.2. Presentation skills", "1.3. Oral Communications" (depending on the requirements for the position you have specified in Module 2 Assignments).*
5. *In Column 3, for each Key Competency enter 1-2 corresponding Critical Tasks. Critical Tasks are typical activities that you will be expected to perform on the job. Critical Tasks can be used to demonstrate your mastery in performing key competencies. For example, to demonstrate a high level of proficiency in 1.1. Written Communications, you may be required to 1.1.1 Write a Memo or 1.1.2 Prepare an Analytical Report.*
6. *In Column 4, identify a benchmark, standard or a sample of best practice that can be used for skills assessment for each Critical Task. For example, what would you use as a best practice/ standard for 1.1.2 Prepare an Analytical Report task?*
7. *In Column 5, identify a concrete piece of evidence ("artifact") that you can use for assessing your level of mastery in performing each Critical Task against the benchmark. For example, for evaluating your ability to prepare a quality analytical report, you can present a sample report written by you (direct evidence). Or, a testimonial from your supervisor/peer (secondary evidence).*
8. *In Column 6, suggest a method for skills assessment (expert, peer- or self-assessment) and 1-2 appropriate techniques.*
9. *In Column 7, write down the results of your self-assessment. You will need these ratings in Module 4. Please be honest!*
10. *When complete, save this Critical Skills Assessment Tool and submit it in the designated box in Module 3.*

Appendix 4

Assignment A4: Critical Skills Dashboard (CSD) and Total Skillset Score (TSS) Tool Example and Template

MRKT 4050 Career Self-Management and Self-Marketing (© Professor Val Chukhlomin, 2020)

Critical Skills Dashboard (CSD) & Total Skillset Score (TSS) Tool (example only!). Version 2020

	Communication Skills		Interpersonal Skills		Analytical Skills		CCS	IT Skills		Personal Skills	T.S.S.
R	Written	Oral Presentation	Teamwork	Leadership	Quantitative	Problem solving	Cross-cultural skills	Relevant software	Code writing	Initiative, working unsupervised	
1					●						
2	●			●			●			●	
3						●			●		
4		●	●					●			
W	20%	10%	10%	10%	10%	10%	10%	10%	6%	4%	100%
S	10	10	10	5	2.5	7.5	5	10	4.5	2	66.5
A											
P											
G											

R - Rating (1 – poor, 4 – excellent), W – Weight (to reflect the importance of the skill), S – your score for each critical task, A- Advantage, P – Parity, G – Gap

INSTRUCTIONS:

1. *This example is indended to illustrate the use of the Critical Skill Dashboard & Total Skillset Score Tool (used in Modules 4-6).*
2. *Your Critical Skills Dashboard (CSD) is based on your self-assessment results (see Column 7, CSAT, Module 3).*
3. *The first step is to populate the first two rows by entering the Critical Skills Areas and Subareas (key competencies) from CSAT in Module 3.*
4. *The second step is to calculate (or estimate) and enter your ratings for each Critical Skill Subarea (key competency) in rows labelled 1-4. To do so, you'll have to aggregate your self-assessment results (ratings) obtained in Module 3 (Column 7). For example, if the key competency "1.1 Written Communication" includes two elements of competency (1.1 Memo and 1.2 Analytic Report) and your self-assessment results for those elements of competency are 3 and 1 respectively, you'll have to come up with an aggregate rating which is probably close to 2. Then, you enter this composite rating in the table as shown and repeat for all Critical Skill Areas/Subareas. As a result, you'll receive your Critical Skills Profile (the blue circles in the table). Please note that your Critical Skills Profile will be different for each position; also, its accuracy very much depends on your choice of standards/benchmarks and honesty of your self-assessment.*
5. *The next step is to enter weights representing the importance of each Critical Skill Subarea/key competency; in the above example weights are assigned to each key competency (see in row "W"). The total of the weights must be equal to 100%.*
6. *Now, in row "S" you can calculate your Total Skillset Score (T.S.S). Suppose the absolute maximum is 100. For Written Communications, one can – in theory – receive up to 100 x 20% = 20 points. But if your factual rating is close to 2 (out of 4), then you can only score 10 points. If you repeat for all Critical Skills and sum up the results, you will get your TSS (66.5 out of 100 in our example).*
7. *The final step is to visualize your results. Green color is used to mark situations where your performance is close to or above the benchmark; yellow is used to highlight the Critical Skills Subareas where some, may be moderate, improvement is required. Red color is to tell you about the subareas where your skill gaps are severe.*

Probably, you can recall a popular phrase "Build on your strengths!" Don't you think that eliminating your weaknesses might be a better strategy for improving your TSS?

{Self-Assessed} Critical Skills Dashboard & Total Skillset Score Tool template. Version 2020

Student Name: ______________ ______________ Term, Year: ______________

Critical Skill Areas	Critical Skill Area 1		Critical Skill Area 2		Critical Skill Area 3		Critical Skill Area 4	Critical Skill Area 5			T.S.S.
Key Competencies											
R	●	●	●	●	●	●	●	●	●	●	
1											
2											
3											
4											
W											100%
S											
A											
P											
G											

R - Rating (1 – poor, 4 – excellent), W – Weight (to reflect the importance of the skill), S – your score(s), A – Advantage, P – Parity, G – Gap

INSTRUCTIONS:

1. *The first step is to populate the first two rows by entering the Critical Skills Areas and Subareas (key competencies) from CSAT in Module 3.*
2. *The second step is to calculate (or estimate) and enter your ratings for each Critical Skill Subarea (key competency) in rows labelled 1-4. To do so, you'll have to aggregate your self-assessment results (ratings) obtained in Module 3 (Column 7). For example, if the key competency "1.1 Written Communication" includes two elements of competency (1.1 Memo and 1.2 Analytic Report) and your self-assessment results for those elements of competency are 3 and 1 respectively, you'll have to come up with an aggregate rating which is probably close to 2. Then, you enter this composite rating in the table as shown and repeat for all Critical Skill Areas/Subareas. As a result, you'll receive your Critical Skills Profile (you may want to move around the blue circles in the table). Please note that your Critical Skills Profile will be different for each position; also, its accuracy very much depends on your choice of standards/benchmarks and the honesty of your self-assessment.*
3. *The next step is to enter weights representing the importance of each Critical Skill Subarea/key competency (in row "W"). The total of the weights should be equal to 100%.*
4. *Now, in row "S" you can calculate your Total Skillset Score (T.S.S). Using the provided example, calculate scores for each Critical Skill Subarea and sum up the results. This way you will get your TSS.*
5. *The final step is to visualize your results. Use green color to mark situations where your performance is close to or above the benchmark; yellow color to highlight the Critical Skills Subareas where some, may be moderate, improvement is required. Use red color for the subareas where your perceived skill gaps are severe.*
6. *When your CSD_TSS Tool is completed, save it and submit in the designated box in Module 4.*

Now, what can you do with the results of this exercise? In Module 5, you will learn how to build self-promotional strategies based on the green areas. In Module 6, you will develop SMART goals for a 2-3-year skill-building plan to address the red and yellow areas.

Appendix 5

Assignment A5: Self-Marketing and Personal Branding Plan (SMP) Template

Student Name: ______________________ ___________________________ Term, Year: __________________________

1	2	3	4	5	6
Critical Skill Subareas	**Identified advantages in competency elements**	**Description of your competitive advantage/strength (on par or above the benchmark)**	**Action Items for self-promotion**	**Targets**	**Importance, timing**
Example: Written Communications	*Example:* Analytical reports *Rating 3.5 (out of 4)*	*Example:* As reflected by my supervisor/peers, I scored highly in the following categories: -developing a compelling argument; - a superb use of sources; - an exceptional formatting and professional look.	*Example:* 1. Find an avenue for showcasing the mastery of skill. - Create an artifact for LinkedIn; - Create a Functional Resume; - Prepare a pitch for an interview.	Year 1: Rating 4	#1 <add dates here>
	<add>				
	<add>				
	<add>				
<add>	<add>				
<add>	<add>				
<add>	<add>				
<add>	<add>				
<add>	<add>				
<add>	<add>				
<add>	<add>				

INSTRUCTIONS:

1. *This Template is designed to help you develop your Self-Marketing and Personal Branding Plan (in Module 5).*
2. *Your personal SM-PB Plan should be based on the results of your Critical Skill Dashboard (in Module 4).*
3. *In Column 1, enter Critical Skills Subareas (key competencies) that are highlighted green in your Critical Skills Dashboard.*
4. *In Column 2, specify elements of competency (critical tasks) that were rated highly in your CSAT (in Module 3).*
5. *In Column 3, provide a short description for each of your advantages/competitive strengths.*
6. *In Column 4, suggest a list of concrete steps (action items) to amplify, showcase, and communicate your competitive advantages to prospective audiences (employers, recruiters, peers).*
7. *In Column 5, set quantifiable targets in a 1-2-year perspective.*
8. *In Column 6, identify the level of importance of each Critical Skill Subarea for your self-improvement; also, indicate when and how you are going to engage in activities specified in Column 4.*
9. *When finished, save results and submit in the designated assignment box in Module 5.*

Appendix 6

Assignment A6: Skill-Building Plan (SBP) Template

Student Name: ______________________ Term, Year: ____________

1	2	3	4	5	6
Critical Skill Subareas	**Identified gaps in competency elements**	**Description of your skill gap**	**Action Items for self-improvement**	**Targets SMART goals**	**Importance, timing**
Example: Written Communications	*Example:* Analytical reports *Rating 2 (out of 4)*	*Example:* As reflected in the rubric for analytical reports and peer-assessment, I scored low in the following categories: -developing a sound argument, - the use of evidence - the use of formats and styles.	*Example:* 1. Take an advanced writing class, with an emphasis on report writing; 2. Discuss my skills gap with an expert, ask for advice and expert evaluation. 3. Work with a mentor.	Year 1: Rating 3 Year 2: Rating 4	#1 <add dates here>
	<add>				
	<add>				
	<add>				
<add>	<add>				
<add>	<add>				
<add>	<add>				
<add>	<add>				
<add>	<add>				
<add>	<add>				
<add>	<add>				

INSTRUCTIONS:

1. *This Template is designed to help you develop your personal Skill-Building Plan (SBP) (in Module 6).*
2. *Your personal SBP should be based on the results of your self-assessment reported in CSAT (in Module 3) and the Critical Skill Dashboard (in Module 4).*
3. *In Column 1, enter Critical Skills Subareas (key competencies) that are highlighted yellow or red in your Critical Skills Dashboard.*
4. *In Column 2, specify elements of competency (critical tasks) that were rated low in your self-assessment (CSAT, in Module 3).*
5. *In Column 3, provide a short description for each of your skill gaps.*
6. *In Column 4, suggest a list of concrete steps (action items) to address the critical skill gaps.*
7. *In Column 5, set quantifiable targets (S.M.A.R.T. goals) in a 2-3-year perspective.*
8. *In Column 6, identify the level of importance of each Critical Skill Subarea for your self-improvement; also, indicate when and how you are going to engage in activities specified in Column 4.*
9. *When finished, save the form and submit in the designated assignment box in Module 6.*

Appendix 7

Assignment A7: Post-Test Self-Audit

Student:		ID	
Area of Studies:		Concentration	
Term, year:		Instructor	

Task 1: Answer questions 1-8 by indicating your level of agreement on the following statements and provide a brief rationale. Levels of agreement: 1 – "Strongly Disagree", 2 – "Disagree", 3- "Not sure", 4- "Agree", 5- "Strongly Agree".

#	Question	Response ("X")						Brief Comment (Rationale for your answer)
		n/a	1	2	3	4	5	
	After taking the course, I have developed a better understanding of:							
1	Career self-management and career building skills							
2	The employer's ("external") perspective on assessing, scoring, and ranking my skills /job readiness in a competency-based, competitive job selection.							
3	How to use business strategy tools such as SWOT analysis for my personal development.							
4	How to use self-assessment for objectively measuring my level of skills acquisition.							
5	How to use skill assessment tools to estimate my likely scores in a job selection process.							
6	How to use marketing techniques for self-promotion							
7	How to develop S.M.A.R.T. skill-building goals							
8	How to plan, organize, undertake, and monitor my skill-building and self-promotional activities.							

Note: Please answer honestly. The grade for this assignment will be solely based on the timeliness and fullness of your response (do not skip questions!)

Task 2: Answer questions 9-20 by indicating your level of agreement on the following statements and provide a brief rationale.
Levels of agreement: 1 – "Strongly Disagree", 2 – "Disagree", 3- "Not sure", 4- "Agree", 5- "Strongly Agree".

#	Question	Response ("X")						Brief Comment (Rationale for your answer)
		n/a	1	2	3	4	5	
	The course enabled me (or improved my ability) to:							
9	Analyze prospective jobs to better match my skills with the job requirements							
10	Analyze job requirements and clarify the knowledge, skills, and abilities that are required on the job							
11	Identify specific critical skills/tasks/experiences that I need to master/demonstrate to best qualify for the desired job							
12	Identify benchmarks (standards, best practices) that represent the expert level of skill acquisition for my desired job							
13	Using peer- and self-assessment, objectively evaluate my current level of skill acquisition against the specified benchmarks and the likely competition							
14	Based on the assessment results, identify my strengths and competency gaps and clarify professional development needs for mastering the specified critical skills/tasks for my desired job							
15	Set specific, quantifiable targets (S.M.A.R.T. goals) for guiding skill-building activities that will enable me to master the critical skills/tasks at the required level							
16	Effectively organize and manage my skill-building activities to reach the required level of skills acquisition							

Note: Please answer honestly. The grade for this assignment will be solely based on the timeliness and fullness of your response (do not skip questions!)

17	Create an effective functional resume emphasizing my mastery of skills required on the job							
18	Plan and undertake effective self-marketing activities to demonstrate and promote my strengths in skill acquisition at the required level							
19	Effectively utilize social media for self-promotion							
20	Overall, more effectively organize my career planning , skill-building, and self-developmental activities							

Task 3: Answer questions 21- 25 by indicating your level of agreement on the following statements and provide a brief rationale. Levels of agreement: 1 – "Strongly Disagree", 2 – "Disagree", 3- "Not sure", 4- "Agree", 5- "Strongly Agree".

#	Question	Response ("X")					Comment (Rationale)
	This course is:	1	2	3	4	5	
21	Academically sound						
22	Well designed						
23	Useful for professional development and career growth						
24	Worth taking by any student						
25	Well taught by the instructor						
26	**What were the best aspects of this course?**						
27	**Where can we improve?**						
28	**Did you watch course videos? Please provide comments.**	Yes	Now				
29	**Were career self-management tools (E-Portfolio, templates, CSAT, Dashboard, TSS) useful? Please provide comments.**						
30	**Do you plan <u>using</u> some of the methods/tools recommended in the course in real life?**						

Thank you!

Note: Please answer honestly. The grade for this assignment will be solely based on the timeliness and fullness of your response (do not skip questions!)

coursera Catalog Search ca Valeri

Home > Personal Development

Overview

FAQs

Creators

Go to Course

Already enrolled

Preview Course Materials

How to Get Skilled: Introduction to Individual Skills Management (Project-Centered Course)

About this course: Do you want to gain a competitive edge on the job market? Would you like to improve the way that you organize, manage, and present your skills to succeed in a competency-based, competitive job selection? Have you prepared to compete for jobs in the age of AI-powered recruiting?

More

Who is this class for: If you are a working professional taking a range of online courses or Coursera specializations for skills enhancement, this class will benefit you. You will achieve better results if you learn how to measure and monitor the effectiveness of your skill-building activities and focus them on gaining a higher ranking in competitive job selection. Having first-hand experience of a competitive job selection will be advantageous in best absorbing the contents of this course.

Go to Course

Already enrolled

Preview Course Materials

Created by: The State University of New York

Go to Course

Already enrolled

Preview Course Materials

Taught by: Dr. Valeri Chukhlomin, Professor
SUNY Empire State College

Taught by: Amy Giaculli, Coordinator of Student Services
SUNY Empire State College

About the Author

Valeri Chukhlomin is Full Professor of Marketing and International Business in the State University of New York's Empire State College in Saratoga Springs, New York. He has a Ph.D. in Political Economy. Prior to his tenure at SUNY, Professor Chukhlomin was Vice-President, International and Commercial, and Founding Dean of the Faculty of International Business at Omsk State University in Russia. He also worked in Australia as a business trainer and international education consultant. Since joining SUNY Empire State College in 2006, Chukhlomin has shifted his teaching and research interests to online learning. He has published books and articles on international distance learning and MOOCs; also, worked as a consultant in several projects aimed at establishing large-scale online programs in the Baltic States, China, and Russia. In 2016 and 2017, two of his projects were shortlisted for awards by the Wharton-QS Reimagine Education, the world's most prestigious competitive event in higher education innovation. In his academic work, Professor Chukhlomin coordinates online courses in Marketing, teaches a capstone course in strategic management for MBA, and is leading his institution's effort on Coursera®.

Made in the USA
Coppell, TX
31 July 2020

32111320R00092